CALLED TO RESCUE
REAL STORIES OF GLOBAL SEX TRAFFICKING SURVIVORS & THE WOMAN WHO FOUGHT TO LIBERATE THEM

Inspired by the Work of Dr. Cyndi Romine

Copyright © 2013 Good Catch Publishing, Beaverton, OR.

All rights reserved. Written permission must be secured from the publisher to use or reproduce any part of this book, except for brief quotations in critical reviews or articles.

This book was written for the express purpose of conveying the love and mercy of Jesus Christ. The statements in this book are substantially true; however, names and minor details have been changed to protect people and situations from accusation or incrimination.

All Scripture quotations, unless otherwise noted, are taken from the New International Version Copyright 1973, 1984, 1987 by International Bible Society.

Published in Beaverton, Oregon, by Good Catch Publishing.
www.goodcatchpublishing.com
V1.1

Dr. Cyndi Romine has dedicated her life to the rescue of our most innocent population. Her tireless commitment to saving children both at home and abroad is admirable and reflects a true calling on her life. Children are being saved, and life is being breathed back into these victims as a result of *Call to Rescue's* important work!

– Jim N. Grenfell, Executive Director — AWARE, Inc., Author of Deceptions: Exposing the Lures of Child Sex Trafficking and Internet Dangers — School-based Prevention Curriculum

Cyndi truly is "Called to Rescue." It is her life and her passion. I've had the pleasure to walk the streets with Cyndi, both in the States and in the Philippines. She walks up and interacts with people that most of us would cross the street to avoid. What we see as "potential harm," Cyndi sees as "harmed." Cyndi truly sees these people through God's eyes.

– Wynne Wakkila, Director of Fighting Against Sex Trafficking (FAST) and former Administrator of Oregonians Against Trafficking Humans (OATH)

Over the past six years, many of us in law enforcement have been trying to raise awareness of a growing epidemic within our country. An epidemic that most want desperately to deny exists out of the sheer horror of what the possibility of this epidemic represents about our society. It is an epidemic that strips its victims of their basic rights as humans and steals innocence in the most inhumane manner possible. The epidemic is known as sex trafficking.

It is a multi-billion-dollar industry when you factor in that many victims also end up supplying material for the underground porn and child porn industry. The vast amount of money to be made through sex trafficking has caused criminal gangs to enter into this market. They are switching from selling drugs to selling young children and adults for sex. The philosophy being, once you sell your drugs, you have to grow or make more. A person sold into the sex trade can be used over and over and over again.

It is sad that it took so many of our children being abused in such a horrific way before this epidemic began to be recognized. Those of us who spoke about this issue before it was recognized as a problem were often dismissed as just talking about an issue that really was not that prevalent. Thankfully for our kids and our society, there were those who had the courage to not only talk about this insidious crime but who also took action to rescue those being sold as sex slaves.

It is with great respect for the work of one of these courageous guardians of our children that I write these words. Dr. Romine has been on the frontlines of this issue rescuing those being exploited by their fellow man. She has been a voice advocating for this issue to be recognized as the epidemic it truly is and has provided training to those in the law enforcement community, including my agency, on how to recognize this crime. I wish her well as she continues her mission of rescuing our children and raising awareness of the growing sex trafficking epidemic in our country and around the world.

– Ozzie Knezovich, Spokane County Sheriff, Vice President of the Washington Sheriffs' and Police Chiefs' Association, Vice President of the FBI-Law Enforcement Executive Development Association, Chair of the Emergency Communication Board

TABLE OF CONTENTS

	DEDICATION	11
	ACKNOWLEDGEMENTS	13
	INTRODUCTION	17
1	THE MADAM'S PEACE	19
2	HOPE BEYOND THE STREETS	57
3	THE COURAGE TO FIND FREEDOM	89
4	ALL'S WELL THAT ENDS WELL	121
5	CALLING IN THE TROOPS	139
6	THE GIRL ON THE BANK	179
	CONCLUSION	205

DEDICATION

I would like to dedicate this book to my family. They have joined me (i.e., let me drag them) all over the world on stakeouts, at Krav Maga classes (Israeli Martial Arts) and so much more in my fight to help and find children who have been victimized, abused and trafficked. They have cried with me and shared my passion on every level.

My passion and commitment to saving lives is real, but my ultimate passion is my family. You are everything to me. Thank you, family!

To every girl who is still held in bondage: May everyone in the world come to your rescue, and may you find the future you were meant to have.

ACKNOWLEDGEMENTS

I would like to thank Dr. Cyndi Romine for her vision for this book and all her hard work in making it a reality. And to the global sex trafficking survivors of *Called to Rescue*, thank you for your boldness and vulnerability in sharing your personal stories.

This book would not have been published without the amazing efforts of our project manager and editor, Marie Osborne. Her untiring resolve pushed this project forward and turned it into a stunning victory. Thank you for your great fortitude and diligence. Deep thanks to our incredible Editor in Chief, Michelle Cuthrell, and Executive Editor, Jen Genovesi, for all the amazing work they do. I would also like to thank our invaluable proofreader, Melody Davis, for the focus and energy she has put into perfecting our words.

Lastly, I want to extend our gratitude to the creative and very talented Jenny Randle, who designed the beautiful cover for *Called to Rescue: Real Stories of Global Sex Trafficking Survivors & the Woman Who Fought to Liberate Them.*

Daren Lindley
President and CEO
Good Catch Publishing

The book you are about to read
is a compilation of authentic life stories.
The facts are true, and the events are real.
These storytellers have dealt with crisis, tragedy, abuse
and neglect and have shared their most private moments,
mess-ups and hang-ups in order for others to learn and
grow from them. In order to protect the identities of those
involved in their pasts, the names and details of some
storytellers have been withheld or changed.

INTRODUCTION

I could start this book with the words, "It was a hot, humid tropical night ..." and for all the times we have worked overseas, that would be accurate.

But instead, I will start by saying, "As I walked out of the Pussy Cat Club ..."

That ought to get your attention!

After fighting the horror of child victimization, abuse and trafficking for more than 25 years, I never get used to the shocking depravity of man. It angers me. It drives me forward to make a difference in each life that I encounter.

I am continually horrified by the attitudes of the buyers who create the demand. To quote a retired U.S. schoolteacher being interviewed about buying a child for sex: *"On this trip, I've had sex with a 14-year-old girl and a 15 year old. I'm helping them financially. If they don't have sex with me, they may not have enough food. If someone has a problem with me doing this, let UNICEF feed them."* (Quote from *Nefarious*.)

You will read the stories of real girls in these pages — their true stories. Some stories have been retold by *Called to Rescue* leadership just as they were explained to us by the survivors themselves. Their names have been changed to protect their identities, and the stories have been interpreted by professional writers. But these women are real, and their stories are true, nonetheless. They will shock you, haunt you and, I pray, drive you to be informed and involved with *Called to Rescue* and this cause.

"There's a special evil in the abuse and victimization of the most innocent and vulnerable children on earth. The victims of sex trade see little of life before they see the very worst of life, an underground of brutality and lonely fear. Those who create these victims and profit from their suffering must be severely punished. Those who patronize this industry debase themselves and deepen the misery of others."

– President George W. Bush, addressing the U.N. General Assembly, September 23, 2003

The one thing I know is that little girls do not grow up saying, "When I grow up, I want to be a prostitute." They love dolls, Hello Kitty and pink! The sad circumstances in the lives of some forced them into a life that is more horrific than their worst nightmares. Beatings, gang rape and complete loss of themselves, often before their 5th birthday.

– Dr. Cyndi Romine

THE MADAM'S PEACE
THE STORY OF MARIA
LOCATION: USA
WRITTEN BY JOY STEINER MOORE

"You gotta pay me first." I sat down on the edge of the motel bed and crossed my legs seductively. I straightened my new satin blouse and fluffed my brown ponytail with my fingers.

The motel room was the tackiest I'd ever been in. The thin bedspread was stained and filthy; the red carpet was worn and unraveling in patches. There wasn't even a bathroom connected to the room.

This place is shady. Gotta make this one quick.

My "trick," a Vietnamese guy, was busy securing several locks on the inside of the door. I'd never seen so many locks, and I wondered why he was being so careful.

CALLED TO RESCUE

When he was done, he sauntered over with confidence and stood in front of me, stroking my cheek with the back of his hand.

"No. You pay me *first*," I repeated, annoyed. "Can't touch me until you pay." I brushed him off and held out my hand expecting cash. But he shook his head like he didn't understand.

"No speak English," he said with a sneer, pushing me hard to the bed.

I reached up to my neck to protect the gold necklace that Meko, my pimp, had given me for a job well done. I was worried about my blouse, too. It was the prettiest piece of clothing I had ever owned. But the man was already tearing at it, and the threads began to rip.

He's going to rape me!

I scrambled to sit up and fight him off, but he pinned me to the bed. I struggled against him, scratching, pushing, slapping, using everything I had to fight back. Then, with every bit of strength I could muster, I flexed my leg, firmly flung it forward and kicked him squarely in the nuts. The man yelped in pain and stumbled several steps backward into a piece of furniture before falling to the floor.

I wasn't going to wait around for him to recover. My heart pounding, I shot up and darted to the door. My fingers fumbled through the locks, and I hurled the door open, my body nearly flying into the dimly lit hallway.

I ran as fast as I could. As I reached the stairwell, I heard his footsteps behind me. In a mad panic, I whirled

THE MADAM'S PEACE

down the three flights of stairs, slowed only by the awkward doors that required opening on each floor.

When I got to the bottom, I scrambled for the last exit door that led outside. I was almost there when I heard the sound of a firecracker, and a sudden warmth washed over my back.

I've been shot.

But I kept going. I stumbled out the door and into Seattle's Chinatown district, which was alive with people at this time of night. I ran and ran, oblivious to the pain, adrenaline pumping, blood soaking through my brand-new blouse. My tight skirt and high heels made it tricky, but I ran a full 10 city blocks to my hotel, ducking in and out of crowds, my breath coming harder with every step. When I reached the hotel lobby, I waited for the elevator, and when it didn't come, I hoofed it up the stairs.

"Meko! Meko!" I pounded on our hotel room door, nearly collapsing into it. "Daddy, I've been shot!"

※ ※ ※

When I was little, my mom operated a daycare center in the basement of our large home in Federal Way, Washington, a suburb between Tacoma and Seattle. I liked my mom's job because there was always someone to play with, and we kids had lots of fun with our friends.

When I was 6 years old, my mom married Jim, and he legally adopted my two brothers and me. He wanted to study to be a pastor, so my mom closed down her daycare business. In order for Jim to attend Bible college, we moved 2,000 miles away to a duplex near his new school in Texas.

My mom worked two jobs as a waitress to support our family, and one of them was the graveyard shift. She wasn't home to notice when Jim started crawling in bed with me at night, touching me sexually and teaching me how to give him oral sex. Jim was nice to me and bought me anything I wanted. In fact, my brothers were jealous of our relationship and of the attention he lavished on me. Sometimes he would come get me out of school and take me to breakfast or to a movie. He liked taking me to the airport so we could watch the planes take off, and I gave him oral sex in the car on the top deck of the parking structure.

Because of all the attention, I didn't know that what we were doing was wrong. I thought that this was what all little girls did with their daddies, but some of our friends and acquaintances grew suspicious.

"I feel horrible telling you this, but I think there's some inappropriate behavior going on between Jim and Maria," my mom's friend whispered one evening after a friendly get-together.

"No! He's just an affectionate father!" my mom insisted.

"I don't know. She was sitting on his lap, and his hand was between her legs. It just didn't look right."

My mom came to Jim's defense on many occasions, refusing to believe that there was anything improper going

THE MADAM'S PEACE

on, rejecting the very idea that her preacher husband might be a predator. Each time she was approached by a different friend, she ended the friendship, and after being confronted with multiple accusations, we moved back to Washington.

We didn't stay there long. We moved to North Dakota for a while, and when I was 11, I was sent to spend the summer with Jim's parents, my step-grandparents, on their farm. Then it was back to Washington again. The sexual abuse went on for years, and it seemed like every time suspicions arose, we either moved or I was sent away, most likely to ease the tension and take some heat off of Jim for a while.

A month after my 13th birthday, my family decided to spend Memorial Day at the new water park in town. I was really excited about going, but when I went into the bathroom to change into my swimsuit, I saw that I had started my menstrual cycle for the first time.

"You're becoming a woman, Maria!" My mom wrapped her arms around me in a big hug and smoothed the loose brown hairs around my face.

I frowned. I was bummed that I wouldn't be able to get into the water at the water park. I'd have to watch from a picnic table while the rest of the family had a good time in the wave pool and on the waterslides.

That day also marked the end of the abuse. Jim never touched me or came into my room ever again.

☙☙☙

CALLED TO RESCUE

A new wild and rebellious Maria suddenly emerged. I began hanging out with older guys and getting into all kinds of trouble. I'm not sure why, but Jim suddenly started acting kind of funny — distant. One day he came up to my junior high school and pulled me out of class. It irritated me, so I leaned casually against the lockers, crossed my arms and acted bored.

"Listen, Maria, I've got to tell your mom." A pained look passed over Jim's face.

"Okay, tell Mom." I rolled my eyes and, with a quick toss of my hair, went back to class, leaving him standing alone outside my classroom.

When school let out at the end of the day, I headed toward my bus, my backpack bouncing on my back behind me.

"Maria!" My mom waved at me from her car, which was parked behind the school buses.

"Hi, Mom. What are you doing here?"

She waited until we were both in the car before she spoke.

"So your dad told me everything today."

Everything? Really? I doubt that. I rolled my eyes, then stared straight ahead, waiting for her to continue.

"I've got all your stuff packed." She sighed. "You're going to go to a foster home for a while. Your brothers need a father, so ..." She trailed off.

"What? You're kicking *me* out?"

"They have horses there," she added awkwardly, as if even *she* realized how dumb it sounded.

THE MADAM'S PEACE

While I was glad my mom was finally doing something about the abuse, it was too little too late. Charges were brought against Jim, and he had his court date several weeks later. My mother never asked me my side of the story. No one from Child Protective Services ever contacted me or asked me to testify. They made their decisions based on my mom's testimony, which was based solely on whatever Jim had told her, which obviously wasn't much. He was put on probation and didn't spend one day in jail. He didn't even have to register as a sex offender. On the very day the hearing was over, just a month and a half after the initial police report, I was sent home to live with them again.

I was furious. Over the next few weeks, I took my rebellion to the next level. I was still only 14, but I started dating an 18-year-old guy. I smoked weed and cigarettes and got a fake ID, and I had sex with my new boyfriend whenever and wherever we could.

I was sick of living with my family. Jim was always on my case about my behavior, so I started staying at my boyfriend's house on a regular basis. When my friend Tina got pregnant with twins, I dropped out of school and moved to a coastal town with her and her boyfriend to help out as their nanny. We had only lived there for three months when her boyfriend accidentally dropped one of the twins and fractured his skull. All three of Tina's kids were taken away from her the next morning, and since she was living on welfare, I suddenly found myself without a place to live.

CALLED TO RESCUE

I befriended a teenage girl named Tammy who was looking for a roommate. We got an apartment together, and I got a job at a fishery, which was really hard work. When the boats came in, I'd work 18-hour shifts for several days, cleaning and gutting fish, then I'd have a week off before the next boats arrived. Because of the quick turnaround and long hours required when the boats were in, my boss gave all of his employees "cross tops," another name for speed, to keep us going strong.

One of the managers approached me after work one day and asked me if I wanted to party at his place. When we got there, he paid me $50 to have sex with him. I didn't think anything of it except that it wasn't bad money. That was my very first "trick."

☙☙☙

Tammy and I had been roommates for a couple of months when I came home one day to find her music blaring loudly in her bedroom, her Doberman Pincher dog sitting outside the door.

This was unlike Tammy, not the usual scene I found when I came home from work. Despite the throbbing and shaking of the music, our apartment felt eerie, almost cold. Something wasn't right.

"Tammy?" I yelled, trying to be heard over the music. The dog growled at me and stood at attention as if guarding her room.

Desperate and frightened for my friend, I stepped

THE MADAM'S PEACE

closer to the door and pounded on it. The dog barked sharply.

"Tammy, are you okay?"

I turned the knob and inched the door open just a crack. When she didn't answer, I pushed it open farther. My heart stopped and the room fell silent when I saw her, my roommate, Tammy — hanging dead in her closet.

Oh, Tammy. Oh, my God.

The sight of my friend's lifeless, dangling frame was more than I could bear. Her lovely face, usually so alive and vibrant, was ghostly pale and drained of all life. I dropped to my knees in shock. My limbs trembling, my stomach began to tense and turn. I fought back the urge to vomit. The music was still blaring from her stereo on the desk, so I stumbled across the room to turn it off. There on the desk was a note in Tammy's bubbly print, explaining how she was sorry, but she didn't want to hurt her boyfriend.

What? What the hell is that supposed to mean?

I knew I needed to call someone, but I was still trying to process everything. The room was spinning. I really wanted to close the closet door, but at the same time, it seemed wrong somehow.

Tammy's dead. Tammy's dead.

I spotted Tammy's phone and phonebook on her bedside table. I knew her dad worked at Safeway, so I flipped through the pages, my hands trembling, until I found the number.

Calling Tammy's dad was the hardest thing I had ever

done. I had to wait on the line for what seemed like an eternity while they paged him in the grocery store. When he finally came to the phone, I could barely choke out the words. I knew that once I told him, his life would never be the same.

After I hung up with Tammy's dad, I called the police. They came right away, along with the coroner and Tammy's family.

Everything was a whirlwind after that. When the police realized that I was only 14, Child Protective Services came and flew me to Seattle, where they placed me in a group home. My mom drove up from Federal Way to take me to lunch, and while I was gone, somebody went through my stuff and stole all my most prized possessions, including some things Tammy had given me before she died.

I can't stay here. I won't, I thought, as I combed through my remaining belongings.

I ran away that night, spending the night sitting on a bench at a Greyhound station, unsure of my next move. A guy propositioned me for sex, and since I'd done it before, I agreed. We hopped on a city bus and rode it for hours, all the way back to his place in West Seattle. I charged him $100.

The next morning, I caught a bus to downtown Seattle and used the money I'd earned to buy a *Guess* blue-jean miniskirt, a matching blouse and white heels. If I was going to be on my own, I needed a way to make money, and there was only one way I knew how. I was crossing the street at 3rd and Pike when a short black guy approached me.

"What's a pretty young thing like you doing down here on a day like this?"

My eyes grew wide.

"Tryin' to make some money," I responded, placing a hand on my hip.

The man studied me carefully, his eyes traveling over my entire body.

"Do you have a man?"

"No …" I wasn't sure what he meant, exactly.

"Well, you do now."

And that was how I met Meko.

ಌಌಌ

Meko led me to a little restaurant and told me that he could help me make some money.

"Order whatever you want, and I'll be right back." He winked at the wait staff. They knew him, obviously. I wondered how many other girls he had brought there.

I was famished, so I ordered some lunch and a "greyhound," grapefruit juice and vodka. I felt very grown up. They actually served me the drink without needing to see my fake ID. It was a horrible drink, though — much too strong for my taste.

Meko returned about 30 minutes later, and we took a cab to his hotel in Chinatown. We spent the next several hours in his room, talking and smoking crack out of a can.

CALLED TO RESCUE

Eventually, he said he needed to see what I had to offer, so I slept with him and performed oral sex. Satisfied with my abilities, he laid down the rules.

"Never sleep with anyone without a condom," he began. "Always collect the money first. Don't talk to or even look at another black man."

"Okay." I nodded, taking a drag of my cigarette.

He continued his speech, rattling off the information as if he had done it a thousand times. "They call me Meko, but you will call me Daddy. In the next few days, you will meet a girl named Flower. She is the best ho I've ever met, and she will teach you everything you need to know."

Meko stood and walked over to the window. He motioned for me to join him.

"See down there on the corner?" He pointed. "That's the track. You'll charge $15 for head, $20 for a screw or $30 for both. Got it?"

"Yes."

"Okay. And from now on, your name is Sunshine."

I liked that.

❧❧❧

I jumped in and out of cars all day and all night long. No sooner would I hop out of one car than I'd have the next trick pulling me into his. Cars were lined up waiting for me. I averaged $250 to $300 a day. I went days without sleep because when I finished turning tricks all night, I'd come back to my dump of a hotel room and smoke crack until sunrise, then go back out to the track to make more money to pay for my room.

Though most of my tricks were older white men, I slept with guys of almost all nationalities: Asian, Hispanic and Indian — everyone except for black guys. I followed Meko's rules to a T. I couldn't even look at another pimp. If I made eye contact, it was telling that pimp that I was interested in what he had to offer me.

I found other girls for Meko, too. I brought two or three home for him and gradually pushed Flower out with all my success. She was jealous of the money I made, and since she was more into her drugs, I quickly replaced her as Meko's "bottom bitch."

One evening, after about two or three months, I was unusually busy, so I stopped by the room to drop off all my money. There on my bed was a note from Meko. It read: "You did good. Stay in for the night." Next to the note lay a beautiful satin blouse and an expensive necklace. The blouse was white and cream-colored with silver and black vertical stripes and a heart-shaped neckline. The necklace was probably worth around $400. They were the most beautiful gifts I had ever received, and they were *mine*. I touched them each delicately, my heart warmed by Meko's kindness.

I quickly changed into the new top and carefully clasped the necklace around my neck. I stood for a minute, admiring my reflection in the dressing table mirror. My brown eyes peered back at me curiously. I looked *older* — much older than my 14 years. Mature. I reapplied my lipstick and pulled my light brown hair into a tight ponytail. Turning back to the bed, I grabbed Meko's note and scribbled a response on the back of it: "I'm having a good night; I'll be back in a while."

Then I took the elevator back to the lobby and headed out to the track, where a Vietnamese guy motioned for me to get in his car. He didn't speak much English, but somehow I understood his request and agreed to ride with him 10 blocks to his hotel.

∾∾∾

"Meko! Meko! Daddy, I've been shot!"

Pain seared through my right shoulder blade as I pounded breathlessly on the hotel room door. I could hear Meko inside, but he was taking a long time to answer.

"Daddy!"

Meko opened the door just wide enough to peek out, and I could tell right away he was loaded with crack.

"Sunshine?" he drawled hoarsely.

"I've been shot!"

"No, you haven't," he said casually, glancing over me.

I forced myself past him and collapsed face-first on the bed so he could see my bloody back.

"Oh, shit!"

Meko ran to the phone and called my regular trick, a cab driver who lived on the same floor as we did. They rushed me to the hospital in his taxi, and the EMTs loaded me onto an ER bed.

THE MADAM'S PEACE

"Please don't ruin my blouse!" I begged, as a nurse began working to cut it off with scissors. "No!"

"Sweetie, it already has a bullet hole in it," she answered gently.

My surgery lasted 13 hours. The man had shot me with a .32-caliber gun, and I learned later that the bullet ricocheted eight times inside my body. When I woke up from the operation, I had staples down my stomach, an ileostomy bag collecting my intestinal waste and a bulb coming out my side from my kidneys. I was a mess.

Two detectives were waiting to talk to me. I told them everything I could remember about the shooter, down to the description of his hotel room and the weird porcelain cat in the corner. The details helped the police track the guy down, and he was arrested and eventually deported.

After 10 days, I was released from the hospital, and my aunt came and picked me up. I stayed for about a week before I snuck out and hitchhiked back to downtown Seattle to find Meko.

After a couple days of work, I realized I was in no shape for it. My wound was fresh and tender, and I still had an ileostomy bag attached to my side. That wasn't attractive to customers. Meko called my stepdad, Jim, to come get me. Jim and my mom were in the process of getting a divorce at the time, so I stayed with him and his girlfriend for three weeks. When I felt good enough to return, I stole all of his girlfriend's jewelry and hitchhiked back to Meko.

For the next two years, we moved from hotel to hotel

all over Seattle. The main track was on Aurora Avenue, and we could charge more out there, like $50 or $60. Because of the ileostomy bag on my side, I never took off my skirt. I just rolled it up, wore a thong and cut a hole in my nylons for easy access.

Meko was everything to me. He bought me everything I could ever want and supplied me with drugs, too. I had gone from eighth grader to streetwalker within a matter of months, but my life with him was what I knew, and I didn't feel like I had any other options. I felt safe under Meko's protection, but that safety was an illusion.

❧❧❧

Rain fell gently on the sidewalk, and I shivered, my skimpy clothing not enough to keep me warm when the weather turned wet like this. I was the only one still crazy enough to be standing on the track on a rainy night. When another chill passed through me, I spun on my heel and headed toward the nearest building in search of shelter.

Suddenly, a large hand clamped over my mouth, and I felt my tiny frame being lifted easily off the ground.

I screamed, but the sound was muffled. The street was empty, not a soul in sight, no one to hear my cries for help. He quickly hoisted me to the curb and threw me in the open trunk of his light blue Cadillac. I caught a glimpse of his face just before the trunk closed: It was Chaz, an extremely tall, well-known pimp who scared the living daylights out of me. As I lay there in the dark,

THE MADAM'S PEACE

shaking and afraid for my life, I racked my brain trying to figure out what rule I had broken — what I had done to make Chaz kidnap me.

When we got to his hotel room, he tied me naked to a chair, my legs splayed open. He sat on the bed, taunting me, his hands holding tight to the leash of his pet pit bull.

"You gonna work for me, Sunshine?"

It was so hot in the room. He must have had the heat cranked up. A bead of sweat trickled down my neck.

"No. I work for Meko." My voice sounded small and timid.

Chaz raised an eyebrow and loosened his grip on the leash. The dog inched toward me, barking.

"Hmmm. Let's try that again. Are you gonna come make some money for me?"

"No." My body shook with fear.

"'Cause if you're not, I'm gonna let my dog eat your stuff." He gave the dog more leeway, until it was standing between my legs, sniffing and barking menacingly.

My eyes grew wide with terror. I shuddered and tried unsuccessfully to scoot the chair backward. But the dog was right there, scarily close to mauling me to death in the worst way imaginable. I didn't see a way out.

"Okay. I'll do it! I'll do it!" my voice screeched. Sweat dripped down my face.

"Good girl, good girl," Chaz sneered.

He dropped me off on the track in Tacoma. I borrowed the phone of the first trick who picked me up and asked him to take me to a Denny's, where Meko came

CALLED TO RESCUE

and got me. Though Chaz continued to work the circuit, we never heard from him again.

☙☙☙

I was sitting in a rickety pickup truck driving to a vacant lot with a trick who had just picked me up. He said he wanted to do it in the bed of his truck, which had a canopy, and he asked me to open the tailgate for him. So I went around to the back and did as I was told.

Just then, out of the corner of my eye, I saw him coming around the side of the truck with a 2x4 raised above his head, like he was getting ready to hit me with it.

Holy shit!

I took off running in the opposite direction, going as fast as I possibly could. I ran across the lot and through a wooded area, losing my shoes in the tall grass. I didn't know where I was going, but it didn't matter as long as I was away from *him*. I kept running, and when I came to the top of a large hill, I rolled down all the way to the bottom, where there was a road. I was sweaty, dirty and barefoot, but I was alive. Panting for breath, I stuck my thumb out and hitchhiked back to my hotel.

Years later, when a well-known Seattle serial killer was arrested, TV news crews showed the man's mug shot with a photograph of his truck and attached camper canopy. That's when I realized that I had almost been another victim of Gary Ridgway, the Green River Killer.

THE MADAM'S PEACE

❧❧❧

The Seattle streets no longer seemed safe for me, so Meko and I decided to make a change. We moved to Portland, Oregon, and opened up an escort service, which was the same line of work, yet just a tad more respectable and organized. We advertised with one line in the phonebook, which meant that instead of hanging out on the streets, I now had to stay in the hotel room next to the telephone, waiting for it to ring. This arrangement bored me to no end, so I got creative, calling taxi services and paying them for referrals. We had heard that the escort service industry was booming over in Hawaii, and my goal was to earn enough in Portland so we could eventually move there.

Finally, after six months, I had saved enough money to pay for airfare and two months' rent in Hawaii. We moved to the island of Oahu, and we changed our names — Meko's to Michael and mine to Tiffany. I immediately started going through the phonebook, calling every escort agency on the island. I got on with the largest one right away, and after a while, I was able to work for all of them. I made $1,000 a night, easily, even with my ileostomy bag still hidden under my skirt.

The owner of the largest escort service became such a meth addict that she could no longer run her business or pay her bills. Michael and I had the money, so we bought her business, and suddenly, we owned the largest escort service on the island. In the meantime, I had brought home some more girls, bringing our total to seven. We had to rent another condo in the same building just to accommodate everyone. We each had a minimum quota of $1,000 per night, which could easily be accomplished by taking four calls at $250 each. We even accepted credit cards.

We were so busy running the service that we didn't have time for fun. I began to take over more and more management functions of the business, so I backed off of my own quota.

I was tired of men and growing tired of Michael. He and I hadn't had sex since we were in Portland. Instead, I started seeing one of our best girls, a Korean named Kristi. I found that sleeping with women was safer, and I felt less abused.

After about a year in Hawaii, I sent Michael on vacation to Vegas to get him out of my hair. He was a crack-head and had become so nervous and twitchy that he needed the curtains drawn all the time. I couldn't even make any noise if we were in the same room. He wasn't the sharpest tool in the shed, anyway; he didn't even know how to write a check. I felt like I, at the age of 18, knew more about running a business than he did. I wasn't doing too bad of a job of it, either.

The company was very successful, and I was able to buy pretty much whatever I wanted. I owned a Porsche and a Cadillac Seville. Money being no object, my walk-in closet was filled with the latest styles. People called me "Tiffany Diamond" because of the necklaces, tennis

THE MADAM'S PEACE

bracelets and diamonds I wore on every finger, most of which came from Tiffany's.

Despite all the money and success, I was increasingly unhappy and extremely bored. I hired a personal trainer in the hopes that exercise might help my mood. I drove around the island over and over, day after day, but I was numb to even the lovely landscape. I sank into a deep depression.

When Michael came back, he brought a girl named Shawna with him. There was a vibe about her I didn't like. I didn't trust her. I sent her back to Seattle after just three days. We didn't know it at the time, but she went directly to the police and wrote a 20-page statement against me saying that our business practices were crooked and that I had collected her money but never paid her.

Things were about to unravel at the seams.

❧❧❧

My girlfriend, Kristi, had never seen snow, so Michael, Kristi, another girl and I planned a ski trip to Stevens Pass, a resort near Seattle. We rented a cabin and spent 10 days on the slopes. It was a wonderful vacation — extremely refreshing after working so hard for so long.

We spent the night before our flight home in a hotel next to the SeaTac airport. The next morning, I cleaned out our rented SUV and took several trips to the dumpster with armloads of trash when I noticed two men following me. I went back up to the room and told Michael.

CALLED TO RESCUE

"There were two guys downstairs who seemed to be watching me and following me."

Michael's eyes filled with fear. He'd had a nightmare the night before that had spooked him, and now he was really scared. He walked over to the window and looked at the parking lot below.

"We need to go," he ordered. "Now."

The four of us loaded all of our bags onto the luggage carts and rolled them downstairs, where we quickly packed the SUV. We piled into the vehicle and had just started the engine when 10 cop cars pulled in and surrounded us from every side.

"Hands on the dashboard! You're under arrest!"

Oh, shit.

❧❧❧

It turned out that, thanks to Shawna's report, the police had been investigating us for months. In fact, during our entire vacation, we had been mingling with detectives in the lobby and the hotel's Jacuzzi and didn't even know it.

Kristi and the other girl were allowed to return to Hawaii, but Michael and I were taken to jail. There were prostitution charges against us in both Seattle and Portland. Since we were co-defendants, we weren't allowed to talk to each other. I had no idea what was happening to Michael. They dropped the charges in Seattle, but in Portland, they offered me a plea deal if I

THE MADAM'S PEACE

would turn over evidence against Michael. I refused. I didn't believe that they would really drop the charges. I should have taken the deal: Michael did and only served six months, while I spent the next two years in prison.

I went through a treatment and rehab program aimed at helping women who had been involved in prostitution. I was able to complete my GED, however, and I was extremely proud of that. I had a steady girlfriend during my two-year prison stay, as well. I was done trusting men. Regardless of the changes I made in prison and through rehab, prostitution was still what I knew best, so despite the instructors' best efforts, I couldn't believe their insistence that I had other options. I just didn't buy it.

When I was released in January 1991, I was 20 years old. After a month in a halfway house, I moved in with a female acquaintance, and we lived in a room in a junky, rundown house with a community kitchen and shared bathroom. I had done a lot of drugs in my time, but I had not yet tried meth. I spent the next six months in that hell hole snorting meth whenever I could. It didn't have the rush that crack did, and it hurt my nose, but that didn't stop me. After being up for a month, I decided to try shooting it in my arm.

Two days later, I woke up with the needle still in my arm, and I was higher than I had ever been in my entire life. It freaked me out. I knew I was spiraling out of control.

Never again. Never again!

I knew how to get clean, but I had never wanted it

before. Now I did. I knew the first step was to get away from Portland and all my friends and connections there. I packed up my clothes and my cat and hopped on a train to Seattle. For some reason, I decided I needed to find Michael.

༄༄༄

When I found him, he was holed up in a tiny studio apartment in downtown Seattle with a girl named Penny. He drove a piece of crap car and went by the name of Steve. He had *nothing*. After all we had built together — the cars, the houses, the jewelry — I was angry. I had just spent two years of my life in prison for this man, and here he had been out and free and hardly had a dime.

That's when it hit me. He couldn't run the business on his own. I was the brains of the operation. He was nothing without me. I decided it was time to make a break from him.

Within six months, I had earned my adult entertainment license and moved to Anchorage, Alaska, where prostitution was legal at the time. I leased the largest in-house massage parlor and club in the city. It had 13 rooms.

We were popular among oil field workers and fishermen who would come through Anchorage before flying home. In Alaska, residents are given a large tax dividend in September, so Native Americans would come to the city to spend their checks on supplies for the winter.

THE MADAM'S PEACE

They'd blow their money in a couple of days, smoking crack and hanging with my girls, and that was how I made my fortune. I no longer worked myself, but I had between seven and 10 girls on staff at a time. I recruited girls from all over the United States. Since we were open 24 hours, the phone rang constantly. I was the "madam," and I had so much money it was running out my ears.

One day a beautiful teenage girl with long black hair came into the club to apply for a maid position. Her name was Lacey, and she was gorgeous.

"You don't want to be a maid," I told her. "I can help you make a lot more money."

In addition to "turning out" Lacey as one of my girls, I was also very attracted to her, and we moved in together. I thought I was in love. I didn't make her pay agency fees, and I let her do whatever she wanted.

As I continued to run my business, I became more unhappy at my core. I hired lovely young girls to work for me — they were innocent and naive, but the work was stealing something away from them.

"Just watch," I'd tell Lacey. "Give them a couple of weeks, and they won't look so beautiful."

Sure enough, after a month or so, they looked old. Used up. Sad and lonely. I even watched it happen to Lacey, and as I looked back at my own life since I was 14, I could see how it happened to me. I had never really had a childhood. From the start, my relationship with men was based on them rewarding me for what I could do for them. I saw it in the way Jim had bought me everything I wanted in exchange for blow jobs. I saw it with the satin blouse, necklace and countless other things Meko bought for me over the years. And now, the tables had turned.

I was the pimp, the madam, turning innocents into whores.

❧ ❧ ❧

"Who were you with? Tell me!" Lacey's face was beet red with anger, and I ducked as she threw a vase across the room, narrowly missing me before it shattered against the wall.

"Nobody! I was at the club!"

"I don't believe you!" she screamed.

"You can ask anyone," I replied calmly. "The phone was ringing off the hook all night long. Besides, if I'm not there, they steal from me. You know that!"

I walked forward and put my hands on Lacey's shoulders. She buried her face in her hands and shook with sobs.

"Listen, if this is going to work, you have to be able to trust me," I tried gently.

The truth was that I was physically and mentally exhausted. The club was wearing me thin. I was there almost 24 hours a day just to make sure things kept running and nobody stole from me. I also had a drug dealer approaching my girls in the club parking lot, and I had to keep getting my security team to kick him out. I had all the money I could ever want, and I had nothing

THE MADAM'S PEACE

more to buy. There was nothing else I wanted. Meanwhile, Lacey had become almost insane in her jealousy. She was possessive and violent, and she wasn't fun anymore. I decided something needed to change.

A few days after my 27th birthday, I gave the club back to the property manager. I broke up with Lacey and moved into a penthouse. I was ready to start a new life.

તેતેત

My new condo overlooked a parking lot near the club, and one evening I noticed some commotion going on outside. Grabbing a blanket, I went out and watched from the balcony as one of my former girls was loaded into an ambulance.

"Hey, there!" my neighbor called out from his balcony, which was next to mine.

"Hi, Ronnie. Do you know what's going on?" He often did.

"She OD'd on cocaine is what I heard."

"Oh, no." My heart sank. I shivered and wrapped the blanket around my shoulders. I lit my cigarette as Ronnie and I silently watched the ambulance turn on its sirens and drive away toward the hospital.

I was about to go back inside when a tall, attractive black guy caught my eye. He was standing below, talking to some of the other bystanders.

"Who's that?" I pointed.

"Him? Oh, that's my boy, Nick."

"You'll have to introduce me," I muttered with a wry smile.

"Will do!" Ronnie grinned.

I waved goodbye to him as I stepped back inside my penthouse.

Since I had been the town's madam for so long, booty calls were easy to set up. I was pretty much able to pick and choose who I wanted. I'd text someone, he or she would come over, and when we were done, I'd send him or her on their way.

A few minutes later, my cell phone rang.

"Hi, is this Maria?" His voice was deep, yet gentle. My heart pounded a little.

"This is she."

"Yeah, Ronnie said you wanna hook up?"

"Right. Sure."

"How about I come over in an hour?"

There wasn't much time. I swung through my house, clearing the clutter and straightening my sofa cushions. Then, with a half hour to spare, I went and bought some groceries. I honestly didn't know what had gotten into me. I had never cared so much about impressing a guy.

We had a wonderful evening together, and even after the sex, we stayed up talking into the wee hours of the morning.

"So, I'm wondering if you'd like to do this two or three times a week ..." I began, trying to feel him out and see if the relationship was still strictly business.

Nick held my gaze steadily, peering deep into my eyes.

THE MADAM'S PEACE

"I'll do it seven," he answered, completely serious.

My heart skipped a beat.

I had never let a man spend the night before, except for Meko. It was one of my rules. But the next morning, I woke up in his arms.

I cooked him breakfast, and we were together from that moment on.

◈◈◈

As I got to know him, I learned that Nick was the big-time dope dealer in town. In fact, he was the one that I had security kick off my property at the club. I thought it was an interesting coincidence that the big-time madam was falling for the big-time dope dealer, but it was absolutely true. I was in love with him. He had such a gentle heart and a sweet spirit; he was unlike any man I had ever met. I was amazed that after all I had done in my life, he loved me, too.

Six months later, we moved to Seattle for a fresh start. We made a decision that we wanted a different life for ourselves — one that didn't include selling sex or drugs. But because neither of us had legitimate work history or education, it was hard to know what places would hire us. After learning how to drive a manual transmission in one night, I got a job as a delivery driver, and Nick detailed cars and planes. He had a drinking problem, though, which affected his ability to hold down a job.

I discovered I was pregnant, which was a complete

surprise, since I didn't think I could have kids because of all I had endured, physically and emotionally. When our beautiful son, Damien, entered the world, he became the most important thing in my life. I felt like the blinders over my eyes were gone, and I could suddenly appreciate the wonderment and innocence of youth. I hadn't gotten to experience that before, and I was determined to do the best I could to preserve that for my baby boy and maybe try to recreate it for myself.

My mom and I reconnected, and I really liked her new husband, who seemed more like a dad to me than Jim ever had. Two weeks after Damien was born, we moved to Tacoma to live near them. I opened a mobile ice cream shop on the side, which was something I had always thought would be fun. My mom told me her church was having revival services and that it might be a good place for me to sell ice cream, before and after church each night. Every evening for six months straight, I drove my ice cream truck to the church and parked it next to the entrance. Since I was there, I decided that I might as well go inside.

The first night, I was shocked by the complete peace I felt when I walked into the church. Even though I was trying so hard to clean up my life, there was still so much chaos inside my heart. When I sat in the pew and listened to the singing, my burdens seemed to lessen somehow. I was still so exhausted from the whirlwind my life had been to that point, but there was something about being in a church that made me feel clean and renewed. Maybe I

THE MADAM'S PEACE

didn't have to work quite as hard at cleaning up. Maybe God could help me.

One particular evening, I was short on cash for gas money and thought that maybe I should just stay home, but I felt such a strong sense that I was supposed to go and trust God to take care of me. So I went, anyway, pulling into the parking lot on fumes, not sure how I would get home. The service was amazing that night, and as the worship leaders sang on the platform and led us in singing to God, I saw beautiful angels appear in the air behind them! All of my doubts disappeared in that instant.

Later, at the end of the service, a woman walked up to me and slipped a $20 bill into my hand.

"The Lord told me to give you this," she said quietly. My mouth dropped open in disbelief.

Gas money from God.

I had grown up in church, but with everything Jim had done to me, I had never really felt close to God before. But now I did. I invited him to take over my life. It was such a good feeling knowing that I didn't have to be in control anymore. He had proven that he could take care of everything in my life, both big and small. I could hardly wait to go home and tell Nick.

☙☙☙

Nick and I both accepted Jesus as our Savior, and we knew the first thing we needed to do was to get our relationship right with God. We got married in 2004 and had the church wedding of my dreams. I wore white, symbolizing the purity God had restored in my heart. I had no actual memories of the countless individual sexual encounters I had experienced or of any of the details regarding them. It was like God had wiped the slate clean and taken those memories away from me. Financially, I was as broke as I'd ever been in my life, but I was happier than I ever imagined I could be.

Over the next two years, however, I had two pregnancies that ended in babies who were born three months premature. Both of the babies passed away. We were heartbroken. The doctor determined that the losses were due to an incompetent cervix, and in 2006, he convinced me to see a specialist who could perform a cervical cerclage. I got pregnant again and had to be on strict bed rest for the majority of the pregnancy. My beautiful princess, Nevaeh, was born early but healthy, and I knew her life was nothing short of a miracle from God.

I had earned my commercial driver's license at a technical school, so I began driving trucks for a living. Nick's old drinking and drug habits had unfortunately landed him in prison, so I was acting the part of single mom for a while. I lost my job in a company buyout and was very excited when I was quickly hired sight-unseen for a driver opportunity in Vancouver, Washington. I packed up all our belongings in a U-Haul and drove away from Tacoma, ready to start a new life. My church's pastor even told me of a church in Vancouver that he thought I would

THE MADAM'S PEACE

like. I was confident God was in control, and I was excited about the opportunities that awaited me.

We were almost to Vancouver when I received a call on my cell phone that I had been disqualified for employment due to my criminal history.

Oh, no. What am I going to do now?

I had already lined up our housing and paid the rent in advance, but now we were in a new city with no friends or family, no support system, no job or foreseeable income. I was a basket case with worry.

On Sunday morning, bright and early, I headed to the church my pastor in Tacoma had told me about. As soon as the doors opened, I tracked down Pastor Greg and his wife, Dr. Cyndi. I poured out my life story, holding nothing back. They accepted me with open arms and promised to help in any way they could. I could tell there was something else on Dr. Cyndi's mind. Her eyes were alive, and it was obvious that the wheels were turning in her head.

"Did you know that I have a ministry to help free girls from sex trafficking in the Philippines?"

"No. Really?" I had no idea.

"Maria, the story about your background — the sexual abuse and prostitution — I don't think it's a coincidence." Her eyes sparkled. "*God* put us in each other's lives."

Dr. Cyndi told me more about her organization, *Called to Rescue*, and her recent desire to expand the calling to help local girls caught up in sex trafficking and prostitution in Portland and Vancouver. I knew as well as she did that some girls never made it out of a life like mine, and even if they did, there was no place for survivors to heal and gain the life skills to move on. As Cyndi and I talked, I grew excited at the prospect of working alongside her to help free other women from the horrific lifestyle that had entangled me for so long.

God can use me. The thought was exciting. Up until that point, I had just been grateful that he had freed me, made me clean and given me a new life. Now I realized that he wanted to go one step further and *use* me to help others do the same.

I began to understand that *this* was the reason God had moved me here. My previous pastor had not known anything about my background or the details of Dr. Cyndi's ministry, and yet somehow everything had fallen into place.

God had orchestrated everything according to his amazing plan.

☙☙☙

I got a job with a temp agency as a driver, and life became settled for a while. Nick got out of jail and joined us, but after a DUI, he had to go back to jail for nine more months. I loved my husband, but there was still a lot of addiction baggage we were working through.

In 2008, I was on the job and pulled my truck off the highway at a checkpoint for a mandatory inspection.

"Uh, ma'am?" The officer studied his computer screen.

THE MADAM'S PEACE

"Yeah?"

"Well, it looks like there's a warrant for your arrest."

"What? There's no way!" I was floored. I had been clean for years.

"You're going to need to call your boss and have them come get the truck."

It turned out that the warrant was from 1991, when I was first released from jail and moved to Seattle. I had told my parole officer I was moving and had gotten permission to leave, so I was sure it all had to be a misunderstanding.

For the next 45 days, I remained locked up. My kids stayed with a friend of mine, and Dr. Cyndi and *Called to Rescue* worked as advocates on my behalf. Apparently the case was complicated by the fact that I had not registered as a sex offender, which I didn't know was required.

They assigned me a new parole officer, and when I met her and explained my case to her, she dug a little deeper for me. I was out of jail the very next day. Three months later, I received a letter dismissing my case. I was free and clear!

Over the next several years, I continued raising my beautiful children, working and running my ice cream truck. With Dr. Cyndi's support, my life began to stabilize. I began helping *Called to Rescue* with individual cases of girls where Dr. Cyndi believed sharing my story might make a positive difference. Several times, I invited girls to come live with me, and I worked with them to get jobs and learn basic survival skills in the real world. My home even served as a safe haven for a pregnant teen whose pimp had threatened to make her have an abortion. It was rewarding to know that instead of "turning innocents into whores," as I once had done, I was now helping girls heal from their hidden pain and scars, giving them a real chance at a new life.

We knew there was a way out, but each girl had to have the internal fortitude to make the decision that she wanted a different life for herself. And when she made that choice, we were there to help, building relationships and a support system that would last a lifetime.

❧❧❧

"Ice cream for sale! Ice cream!" My kids giggled and waved at the children on the beach as Nick tied our boat to the dock. Dozens of swimmers waved back enthusiastically and ran through the sand to their parents to ask for money.

Ever since we had invested in the ice cream boat, Damien and Nevaeh begged us to take it out nearly every day. So, donning our lifejackets, and with the wind blowing through our hair, we'd cruise up and down the river, stopping at all the popular swimming spots with our offer of ice cream bars and other delicious treats.

It was something that made me truly happy, providing such a simple pleasure of life to others. It was therapeutic for me, too, helping me to recapture some of the childhood joy I had been denied.

The kids lined up, cash in hand. One by one, I took

THE MADAM'S PEACE

their orders, while Nick and our kids doled out the ice cream treats.

"Thank you!" a little girl said, accepting her pink strawberry bar and looking up at me gratefully with chocolate brown eyes. Her brown ponytail bounced and swayed with the light wind.

"You're welcome, sweetie," I replied, a smile crossing my lips. I couldn't help but notice how much she reminded me of myself at that age.

When the line was through, Damien packed up our sign and crawled back into the boat, while Nick untied the boat from the dock.

"Ready, everyone?" I glanced over my shoulder at my son and daughter, squeezed in tightly next to the ice cream cooler.

"Yep!" the kids chimed in unison.

"Well, then, let's go!" True happiness filled my heart.

Nick turned the key in the ignition, and off we sped across the water, headed for our next adventure wherever the waterway might lead.

One humid, hot night with the gutter smells hitting me as I got out of the van, I saw a girl about 20 years old. Her makeup wasn't particularly heavy, not like the girls that surrounded her. It was more that she was dressed provocatively.

I walked up and put my arm around her. She heaved a big sigh and sank into my arms, as if saying, "Maybe I won't have to do this tonight. Maybe 'rescue' is here."

The pimp came toward us, and I was in the van and gone.

Two nights later we were headed for another red light area, but I said, "I have to go back! I need to find that girl." We stopped the van, and I thought, Man, I hope I can find her! Suddenly, she was right in front of me.

With neon lights flashing and girls beckoning customers, I looked at her and said, "Tonight I came back. Just for you!"

With tears in her eyes, she replied, "Yes. Thank you!"

Plans were made for her pickup and the beginning of her recovery and new life.

HOPE BEYOND THE STREETS
THE STORY OF CARISSA
LOCATION: USA
WRITTEN BY KAREN KOCZWARA

What have I gotten myself into?

Tears streamed down my cheeks as I tried to keep from screaming out. The ropes rubbed into my skin as he circled around the chair.

What did I do to deserve this?

"If you try to leave, I'll go find your family and kill them," he hissed, his eyes boring into mine.

No! No! My heart thudded in my chest as I tried to keep calm. I watched in horror as he pulled a hair-bleaching kit out of the plastic bag and spilled out the contents.

No! What are you doing to me?

Utter fear gripped me as my eyes darted around the hotel room. I contemplated escape, but I knew it was no use. He'd taken all my valuables, including my money, identification and phone. I was now a nobody, a helpless victim at his mercy. And I was about to be sent out to work the streets.

❧❧❧

HOPE BEYOND THE STREETS

My childhood was nothing out of the ordinary. Like most little girls, I spent my early years playing with dolls, twirling in pretty dresses and dreaming of one day becoming a princess. I was an only child until age 7, when my brother came along. As I entered my teenage years, I dove into volleyball, gymnastics and choir. Though my parents stayed married, they fought regularly, and I often heard screaming down the hall at night. My father was the disciplinarian, while my mother assumed the role of a friend. When I got in trouble, my father sharply reprimanded me. Only after he did his fair share of yelling did he offer a hug and mumble an "I love you." He rarely came to my sporting events, and I felt like somewhat of an afterthought as the years went by.

While most of my friends began going out to parties in high school, my parents enforced a strict curfew and forbade me from leaving the house. Their attempts to shelter me backfired when I turned 16. I got a car and, along with it, my first taste of independence. I began hanging out with a rough crowd, became sexually active with boys and started smoking pot. Though I did fairly well in school, I dropped out my senior year after I began seeing someone seriously. I regretted my decision right away but decided to continue on the path I'd chosen. I landed a job as a cashier at Walmart and secured my own apartment. I continued dating my boyfriend and distanced myself from my family.

One night, we got into a huge argument. I called a girlfriend and asked her to pick me up. "Let's go dancing,"

CALLED TO RESCUE

I suggested, eager to get out of the house. I slipped on a cute outfit and waited for her to arrive.

Another friend of ours dropped us off in downtown Seattle. When we arrived at the club, we discovered, to our disappointment, that it had been shut down for remodeling.

"What now?" I sighed. "How are we gonna get home?"

"Let's take the bus home," she suggested.

We boarded the public bus, but after climbing off a bit later realized we'd gotten off at the wrong stop. I knew we'd landed in one of the shadiest areas of Seattle. Homeless people huddled against dilapidated buildings, eyeing us as we walked by in our shiny dance club attire. My pulse began to quicken as I wondered how we'd find our way home.

Suddenly, a shiny SUV drove up. A good-looking guy in his mid-20s rolled down his window and smiled. With dark skin, jean shorts and a hat, he seemed harmless enough. "You girls need a ride home?" he asked.

"No, we're good," my friend replied quickly, tossing me a wary glance.

"It's okay," I whispered. I turned back to answer the handsome driver. "Thanks, we'd love a ride home."

"All right, climb in! I'm Terence, by the way."

My friend reluctantly climbed in the car with me, and we drove off. Terence stopped at a 7-Eleven and bought a cheap bottle of wine. We then went back to my apartment, and I invited him in. After popping open the wine, we began chatting.

HOPE BEYOND THE STREETS

"You are really beautiful, you know that?" He leaned forward on the couch, staring into my eyes. Up close, he was even more handsome and alluring. Though casually dressed, his fancy car led me to believe he was not hurting for money.

I blushed, flattered by his words. "Thanks," I mumbled.

My friend went home, and I continued hanging out with my new admirer into the early hours of the morning. The next day, he called and asked to see me again. We began spending time together, and he acted like my new boyfriend. As he continued to flatter me, I fell under his spell, convinced we had something special. One day, he asked if I'd like to go to Portland with him for the weekend.

"That sounds cool," I agreed enthusiastically. Spending an entire weekend away together with the guy I was falling for would be an exciting reprieve from my mundane life.

I called my work and told them I'd be gone for a few days. When we arrived at the hotel in Portland, Terence told me to leave my bag of clothes in the car. I followed him into the hotel room, eagerly awaiting the romantic plans he had in store for me. He quickly closed the door behind us. I spun around, expecting one of Terence's passionate kisses.

Instead, he grabbed me firmly, tied me to a chair and pulled out a Sally's Beauty Supply bag.

"What are you doing?" I cried, fear gripping me as he knotted the rope tightly around my body.

CALLED TO RESCUE

"Shh. Don't try anything funny. If you try to leave, I'll go back and kill your family," he hissed, his eyes now darkly sinister as they bore into mine.

He grabbed my purse, dumped out the contents and took my credit cards, social security card and anything valuable. He then removed the beauty supplies from the bag and proceeded to bleach my hair. I sobbed quietly, terrified as a hundred thoughts raced through my mind. My heart raced, and I began to shake as the tears trickled down my cheeks. *What have I just gotten myself into? What have I done to deserve this?* Tempted to let out a scream, I bit my bottom lip and tried to remain calm. My Terence, who I thought I was falling for, a romantic, sincere suitor sweeping me off my feet just hours ago had now transformed into a heartless monster as he charged around the room. *He's serious. He could go back and kill my whole family if I don't do what he says. I've gotta play it cool.* Though I wasn't very close to my family, I still loved them, and the idea of anyone harming them was unbearable, especially on my account.

When he was done, Terence tossed me a short skirt, a tank top and a pair of shoes. "Put these on," he instructed as he untied me.

My hands trembled as I slipped into the clothes. I kept my eyes cast downward, not wanting him to see the terror in them. He'd seemed so kind when he'd offered me a ride and so sweet and attentive on our subsequent dates. I'd never suspected he had evil motives. What did he plan to do to me now?

HOPE BEYOND THE STREETS

I looked around the hotel room, wondering if I could make a quick escape. But I knew there was no use. He'd taken all my money and my phone. I was now at his mercy. *Just do what he says, Carissa. You'll figure something out.*

He led me back to the car and headed to 82nd Street, where he drove up and down a dimly lit street. "Here's how this goes," he explained. "You can't go past these certain streets, got it? If any other pimps pull up next to you, do not make eye contact with them. Do not speak to them. This is very important. If they approach you, run away. Otherwise, they'll think you belong to them."

I gulped hard and nodded. *So I'm a prostitute now. And Terence isn't my boyfriend. He's my pimp! He's going to put me out on the streets and pimp me out, just like that. What have I done?*

"When johns pull up to you, ask them to unzip their pants. There are a lot of undercover cops cruising around here, and if it's a cop, he won't reveal himself to you. If they won't do as you ask, just walk away. Make as little conversation as possible. You don't want to waste time. Just do your business and get back out on the street so you can start making more money."

I nodded again, blinking back tears. My eyes darted around the dark streets as I wondered if I could attempt an escape here. I remembered my family back home and the threat he'd made. *He'll kill them. He's not going to let me go that easily. I have to just suck this up and do what he says.*

"Oh, and one more thing," Terence added as he opened the car door. "I'm not gonna pick you up unless you've made $1,000."

A thousand dollars. I gulped again. That was more than I brought home from Walmart in two weeks. How was I going to rake in that sort of money in one night?

I climbed obediently out of the car and walked down the sidewalk, teetering in my heels as the cars drove by. Several cars stopped and honked, but I remained frozen to the ground, afraid to approach anyone. When Terence finally picked me up, he grew furious.

"I told you to make $1,000!" he barked, slapping me across the face. "What happened?"

"I'm sorry. I'll try harder," I stammered. "Just give me a chance."

He slapped me again. "You better make your quota, or you can expect more of this," he sneered.

After a beating, we returned to the hotel. A week later, he announced we were leaving for California. I fell asleep in the car, and when I awoke, I discovered we'd arrived at a big house in the middle of nowhere. There were no gas stations, stores or other houses around — only open fields. *I guess there's nowhere to run to,* I realized, my heart sinking.

Terence punched in the gate code, and we drove inside. After walking through the doors, I discovered several other girls who looked about my age. They looked me up and down but said nothing as he escorted me upstairs. Several bedrooms lined the hallway, each bearing locks on the outside of the doors. As I stepped inside a room, I noted the bars on the windows. *No chance to escape. He thought of everything.*

"Take a shower. We're gonna leave in a bit," Terence instructed.

Where are we, and what sort of crazy place is this? I wondered as I stripped off my clothes.

After I showered, Terence instructed me and another girl to get back in his car, and we sped off. Soon, the barren fields turned into city streets, and after a while, signs for Los Angeles popped into view. We eventually arrived in Anaheim, home to Disneyland, "The Happiest Place on Earth." He dropped the other girl off in one area and me in another. I stepped out of the car and onto the dirty street, fully aware of what I had to do. *I have to meet my quota. And I can't talk to other pimps.*

My wobbly legs propelled me to the edge of the sidewalk, where I began to walk up and down. I eventually got the hang of things, and slowly, the money rolled in. But if I did not make my nightly quota, Terence left me on the street.

"You'll come back when you've made your money," he told me firmly.

When I returned, he searched my entire body thoroughly to make sure I hadn't hidden any money. If I returned empty-handed, he beat me and threatened to kill me. This terrible cycle went on for weeks.

On occasion, Terence left me alone in a hotel room. I considered running, but I didn't know where I'd go or what I'd do. I had no money or identification on me. I couldn't even get a bus ticket if I tried. I'd been dumped off in an unfamiliar place where I knew no one except my pimp, and I was not sure who to trust. Terence forbade me from even making eye contact with a stranger at a stoplight. If I ran, he would most likely find me and hurt me or my family. It was not worth the risk. I felt trapped.

One night, I noticed another pimp trying to follow me as I worked the streets. I walked faster, but he continued to follow me. I ducked behind a building, trying to hide, but he didn't let up.

"Why are you letting him follow you?" Terence asked after calling my cell phone.

"I'm trying to get rid of him," I insisted.

"Go into a grocery store," he instructed.

I did as he said, my heart racing as I tried not to draw attention inside the store. A few minutes later, Terence showed up, walked up behind me and kicked me swiftly in the butt. Everyone in the store stopped and stared at me, but no one did anything. Tears pricked my eyes and rolled down my cheeks. *Everyone's staring at me, but no one's offering to help,* I realized, embarrassed and angry. *They have no idea who I am.*

"You need to get back outside," Terence snarled.

I obeyed and walked back outside, trying to compose myself.

"I am gonna go check on the other girl," Terence told me. "You get back out there, you hear me?"

I nodded and headed back toward the street. When he

was out of sight, I ducked into a bus stop and sat down. Suddenly, I heard a deep voice behind me. Someone seemed to be discussing purchasing plane tickets with someone. When I glanced back, I saw a black guy ambling toward me from the hill behind the bus stop. It was the other pimp that had been following me.

"Hey, listen, I just want to be your friend," he called out. "I don't want to hurt you."

I grew angry. "You are gonna get me in trouble," I hissed.

"Come on. Just stop for a second and talk to me. I promise. I just want to be your friend," he persisted.

For the first time that night, I stopped to take a good look at him. As I studied his eyes, I wondered if he was sincere. I shuddered, thinking of my other pimp waiting for me down the street. If he discovered I was talking to this guy, he'd be furious. He'd already beat me every night for not bringing home enough money, telling me how stupid and useless I was. But what if this guy was different? What if he really could help me?

"Will you please leave me alone?" I pleaded.

"Technically, I could take you right now. You just talked to me," he snapped.

I peered around nervously and then ran up the hill behind the bus stop and hopped into his car. We began talking, and he shared a little bit about himself. In turn, I told him my story.

"Would you ever hit me?" I asked.

"No, never," he promised. "I only have one other girl. I

could take care of you. I'll treat you well. What do you say?"

I took a deep breath. "Okay, just get me away from my pimp, 'cause he's gonna kill me."

He drove me to the hotel I'd been bunking at, and I raced up and grabbed my belongings. I then hopped in his car, and he drove me to Los Angeles where he'd been staying. The farther away we got from Anaheim, the more easily I began to breathe. *Okay, I think I got rid of Terence,* I thought with relief, glancing behind the car. *I don't think he's going to follow me anymore. Please, let him be gone.*

When we arrived in Los Angeles, my new pimp, Andre, introduced me to his other girl. She told me she was from Canada. "He's cool," she said. "He will let you visit your family anytime you want to. I just got back from visiting mine not long ago."

That's cool, I thought to myself. *Maybe he's more reasonable than Terence.*

I spent the next several months working the streets and truck stops of Los Angeles with my new pimp. Every night, the drill was the same. He parked nearby after dropping me off, and I then walked up and down my designated "track" until a john pulled up. After asking them to reveal themselves, I asked them what sort of service they wanted. A "car date" meant we'd drive to a discreet area and do whatever he wanted for roughly 30 minutes. Most johns preferred to go to a nearby pay-by-the-hour hotel.

HOPE BEYOND THE STREETS

The minute I got into their car, I called Andre and described what sort of guy I was with and what their car looked like. I then texted him the license plate of the car. If I went to a hotel room, I informed him of the exact location and the room number. The routine was to pick a hotel with outdoor-facing rooms so Andre could keep an eye on it from the parking lot.

I also gave Andre an estimate of how long I'd be gone. If I did not come out within the time I'd told him, he called to check up on me. He also suggested I leave my cell phone on the nightstand or put it under the bed in case of an emergency. I often left my phone on speaker so he could hear everything. We agreed that if anything went awry, I'd use a code word, and he would help me escape.

Often, I worked until the sun came up. When I grew hungry, Andre would come and pick me up for dinner. When we got back, he'd pick up his other girl and take her out. One of us remained on the track at all times.

Unlike my first pimp, who'd threatened to kill me if I did not bring home enough cash, it felt like Andre treated me with respect. He made sure I was properly groomed, provided three hearty meals a day and took me shopping for nice clothes. He never once hit me and seemed to take a genuine interest in me. We slept together at his frequent request, and he asked me about my family and my life back home.

"What was your dad like? Did you have a happy childhood?" he asked me.

I told him about my father and how I'd never felt good

enough. He really listened intently, seeming truly compassionate. As the months went by, I began to wonder if I was falling in love with him. I did not realize that he'd later use this information against me, that his affection was all a manipulative act. I was simply an insecure girl who'd been sucked into a dark, dark world, and I convinced myself this was the only life I'd ever have.

To my surprise, the johns who pulled their cars up to the curb were not the typical shady characters one might expect to hunt down a prostitute. Firemen, professional football players, judges, entertainers, teachers, police officers, men who barely spoke English and even gay men made up my clientele. Some of them even wanted to come with their girlfriends or wives. Many did not even want to have sex — they simply wanted to have a few drinks and talk. Some were in the process of a divorce, while others confided they'd been trapped in a lonely marriage for years. Sometimes, we sat on the edge of the bed, sipping wine or beer and chatting until our time was up. I felt sorry for them. But at the end of the night, it was all about the cash. I pocketed my money and returned to Andre, where I handed it over to him. I wouldn't receive a dime for all my hard "work."

I soon turned to drugs, snorting cocaine as an escape. Being high made my lifestyle more tolerable. With a fake name and some drugs in my system, I could easily slip into an alternate world, one where I would try to forget I was just a young girl forced to sleep with men to make a living.

HOPE BEYOND THE STREETS

I moved around Southern California with Andre for a while. He talked of taking me and his other girl to exciting, exotic places like Hawaii and New York. He often took us to Las Vegas. We worked the streets for two nights, sometimes servicing up to 20 clients in one evening and bringing back thousands of dollars. We then spent the rest of the time shopping at the posh stores there and relaxing by the pool. I came back to the hotel with armfuls of shopping bags from high-end stores. *Maybe he really does care about me,* I told myself. *After all, he buys me Coach purses.* I knew a lot of other girls weren't so lucky. They often went without meals and were beaten and neglected. *Things could be worse,* I reasoned. *At least he's looking out for me.*

"No man will ever want you, Carissa," Andre told me often. "You're a whore, after all. You have sex with all these men. Who's gonna want a girl like that? You just stick with me, because no one will ever care for you like I do."

He's right, I decided. *I'm a whore. No guy is ever gonna want to marry me. This is my life now.*

I soon moved from the world of street prostitution to online prostitution. With free Web sites like Craigslist, Andre could post a simple ad and receive plenty of calls within minutes. This opened up a whole new world of possibilities and a brand-new clientele.

Some clients preferred "in-calls," where Andre arranged an appointment for them to come to my hotel. Others preferred "out-calls," where I went to their hotel.

CALLED TO RESCUE

As more and more Web sites began to pop up, business continued to boom. I built up a steady clientele in several cities in California, and many johns became regular customers. Andre remained happy as I kept the money rolling in. Some nights, I brought home as much as $5,000. Long gone were the days of working for minimum wage at Walmart. A closet full of name-brand clothes comprised my new wardrobe. Expensive jewelry and high-end purses were another perk. But this new, lavish lifestyle came with a hefty price tag as the dark world of prostitution stole any remnants of my teenage innocence.

During one of our trips to Vegas, another pimp kidnapped me while I worked the streets. He threw me into the trunk of his car before I could wrestle myself out of his grasp and drove me back to his house. There, he forced me to sleep with him before dropping me back off with Andre. On another night, a Hispanic man pulled me into his car, raped me and then shoved me out of the car without my clothes. Mortified and badly shaken, I ran to the nearest bush and huddled behind it until Andre came for me. Though I had now slept with hundreds of men, these incidents made me feel violated and afraid. Despite the lavish shopping trips, expensive clothes, jewelry and nice meals, I knew my lifestyle was a dangerous one. And while Andre promised to protect me, we both took a risk every night when we interacted with strangers from the streets. One wrong move and we could both wind up dead.

One night, as I worked the streets, another Hispanic

HOPE BEYOND THE STREETS

guy pulled up in a truck. As I approached him, he yanked me into the truck and sped off. He pulled out a large gun. My heart pounded violently, as if it might burst out of my chest as he pressed the cold tip of it against my skull.

I'm gonna die. Right here and now, I'm gonna die. He's gonna put a bullet through my brain, I realized in horror.

"Give me all your money," he hissed.

"I don't have any money on me, I promise," I yelped, shaking wildly as he kept the gun pressed to my head.

He grabbed my purse, my phone and my shoes. After deeming the contents of my purse worthless, he slowed down, opened the truck door and pushed me out onto the asphalt below. I rolled onto the ground, still shaking as I pulled myself up. Barefoot, cold, frightened and disoriented, I stumbled down the road and tried to find my way back to Andre. When at last I reached him, I told him what had happened.

Andre's eyes turned to angry slits. "What kind of car was it? We'll hunt down this jerk!"

But my perpetrator was long gone. While Andre remained visibly upset, he turned me back out on the streets the next day. After all, he had to make a living. I had to make it for him.

I continued to stay with Andre, still convinced that he loved me like no one else. I grew close to his other girl, and we often exchanged stories after coming home from work in the morning. We developed a friendship, and I was grateful for her company. Often, I thought about home, wondering what my family was doing and if they missed me. We hadn't exactly been on the best terms when I'd left home at 18, but I knew they must still think of me. Despite my parents' frequent fighting, they'd still provided a stable home, and now, a warm bed and a familiar face suddenly sounded comforting. I lay awake at night sometimes considering what it might be like to escape. But Andre had stripped me of everything. He now owned me, and I did not have a single dollar to my name. He controlled my every move and knew where I was at all times. Leaving would be next to impossible.

Then everything changed.

While working the streets in Los Angeles, I mistakenly got into a car with an undercover police officer. After quoting him a price for sex, I realized what he was.

"Just let me out of the car, please," I begged him.

"My hotel is just down the road a couple blocks," he said.

"I can't go past this street," I explained, panicking.

He opened the door and let me out of his car. I ran into a nearby gas station and locked myself in the bathroom. Moments later, I heard Andre on the other side of the door.

"The police are outside! You're gonna go to jail!" he cried. "Come on, right now!"

I hopped in Andre's car, and we sped away. "We'll go on the freeway. The local cops can't get on the freeway," he explained.

But just before we reached the freeway near Beverly

HOPE BEYOND THE STREETS

Hills, we heard sirens wailing behind us. I glanced back and saw a trail of police cars just a few yards away. We turned the corner and hit a dead-end road, and my heart sank.

Time's up. They got us. There's no escaping now.

The cops arrested me and Andre and hauled us both to jail. After processing me, the officials told me that my family had filed a missing persons report several months before. "They are worried about you," they told me. "You need to call them."

I made a collect call to my aunt, who got a hold of my parents. I remained in jail until my court date. On that day, my father flew down from Everett. As the judge faced me, she said, "If you leave with your father right now, I will drop the charges. But if you don't, we will have to proceed." She then added, "If I let you go out on your own, you will go right back to this lifestyle. I've seen it all — busted lips and busted ribs, black eyes, drugs. I don't want that to happen to you. Go home with your father."

I took a deep breath. I did not want to go home with my father. I did not want to face my family, friends and everyone back in the Northwest. They would not understand the nightmare I had endured. While they'd sat in their nice houses and led comfortable lives, I'd been forced to fend for mine on the streets. If they learned of the lifestyle I'd led, they'd be horrified and would never accept me again. But as much as I did not want to go home, I also did not want to stay in jail. "I'll go home with my father," I agreed.

Immediately, I thought of Andre. I had not seen him since we'd been arrested. Had he gotten off, or was he still in jail? He'd brainwashed me to believe I could not live without him. I had to find out if he was okay.

When I get outside, I'll run. I'll find him, I decided.

When the judge released me, I stepped outside and saw my father waiting with the public defender, who was prepared to escort me to the car. As I looked into my father's eyes, I began to freak out.

"Calm down, Carissa. It's okay. We're going to go home now. You're going to be all right," my father said gently.

But I came unglued. I turned to the public defender and lunged at her, flailing my arms about as I unleashed a string of horrible names in her direction. She tried to calm me down, too, but I did not want to hear any of it.

"Look, missy, if you try to run, I will escort you right back to jail," she snapped. "So I suggest you cooperate."

They had to hoist me off my feet, the two of them struggling as I thrashed and screamed, and wrestled me into the car. I sat sullenly next to my father, staring out the window as the bustling freeways of Los Angeles disappeared behind us.

"How could you do this?" my father cried. "Don't you know what sort of diseases are out there? What sort of creep would put you up to this? He must be a terrible person!"

You know nothing about what I've been through, I thought angrily. *You don't know that I've been beaten and*

HOPE BEYOND THE STREETS

kidnapped and brainwashed and lied to and pimped out to hundreds of men. You think that somehow I chose this life, that I'm just a whore who ran away from home to sleep with guys. You know absolutely nothing about me.

As my father went on and on, his voice rising, I gripped the seat, trying not to lose control. *Andre said this would happen. He was right. Everything I feared might happen is coming true. My father doesn't really love me. He's never going to forgive me. And no one else will ever love me or understand me the way Andre does. I don't want to go home.*

"You have no idea what I've gone through," I told my father wearily, too emotionally drained to launch into my terrible tales. I rested my head on the seat and tried to fall asleep for the remainder of the long drive home to Everett.

My family was happy to see me when I returned. They'd been worried sick and had filed a missing persons report months before.

I returned to my old bed and tried to acclimate into normal life again, but it was not easy. They had many questions about what I'd been doing for the prior few months, and though I answered some of them, they still remained confused. Why hadn't I just left? Why did I let myself get sucked into such a lifestyle? I couldn't explain to them that I didn't feel I could leave.

No one understands me like Andre, I repeated to myself. *There's no point in trying to make a new life for myself. I need to go back to him.*

I had memorized Andre's phone number long ago. I

called him up and asked him what had happened after we were arrested. He explained that his other girl had bailed him out of jail.

"I'm back home in Everett, but I want to leave," I told him. "There's nothing here for me anymore."

"I'm gonna get you a cab and buy you a plane ticket," he said. "I'll get you back down here."

"Thanks," I replied, relieved to have a plan as I hung up the phone.

Since I'd returned home, my parents had kept me under their watchful eye. *How am I gonna get out of the house?* I wondered. I decided to tell my mother I was going to the mall. "I'll be back in a little bit!" I called out.

As promised, Andre arranged for a cab to the airport and a plane ticket once I arrived. I returned to Los Angeles, and we happily reunited. He immediately put me back on the track, and I returned to "work." But after just a few weeks, he was arrested again and went back to jail. With no one left to watch over me there, I decided to go up to Seattle. *Maybe I should give things another try,* I decided.

I returned to the Northwest, looking for a clean start. Though I had been through hell and back, I also wanted to recreate a sense of normalcy in my life. Perhaps if I steered clear of my family, I could start fresh and forget about my past. I signed up for classes at the local junior college, hoping to secure a degree in Travel and Tourism and with it a better life.

After reconnecting with some old friends, I fell back

HOPE BEYOND THE STREETS

into old patterns. I hooked up with a stranger I met after a night out with my girlfriends. He wanted nothing to do with me, and soon I found myself pregnant, then tackling motherhood alone.

My daughter's birth brought me a chance at a fresh start once again. I landed a job at a local bowling alley and bought a car. Things were less than ideal, but I still held out hope that life would turn around.

Through some mutual friends, I met a new boyfriend, Jason. I soon became pregnant again, and we had a beautiful baby boy. Unlike my daughter's father, he decided to stick around.

As we built a life together and I fell more in love, I decided to be open and honest with him. I sat him down and explained the details of my past. "There's something you should know," I told him quietly. I tried to keep my voice steady as I spilled my shameful secret. "I was a prostitute in California." I laid out the whole story, starting with how I'd made the mistake of going home with the wrong guy one night.

He listened intently, and I hoped from his demeanor that he might be empathetic and forgiving. But instead, he used the information against me. "You know what? I'll take care of you. You're only 21, and you've got two kids. How else are you gonna support yourself? No one else is gonna be with you, but I'll stick around and be your new pimp. What do you say?"

"You're saying you want to be my pimp?" I stared at him, incredulous.

CALLED TO RESCUE

"Well, if you don't want to let me do that, you'll be alone for the rest of your life."

My old beliefs about my worth and my past quickly returned.

He's right. This lifestyle is all I know. Why would I think I could try for anything more? Why bother going to college or trying to get a career when I already know the streets? "All right, I'll do it," I agreed.

After doing some research, I learned that police had cracked down on street prostitution in the Seattle area over the past few years. Online prostitution remained alive and well, however. And dance clubs offered a new way to make good money. Jason, my boyfriend and new pimp, began selling cocaine, and I returned to the world of prostitution.

I walked into local strip clubs and offered my services. In no time, I was up on the stage, scantily clad as I strutted around for the audience. Men of all ages gawked as they threw money at me. I learned that I could also offer private shows. For 30 minutes, men could follow me into a back room without any cameras. There, they could do whatever they liked. Just as I had in Los Angeles, I detached myself from my real self and became another girl. At night, after the kids went to bed, I would snort cocaine to escape.

My boyfriend posted ads online, and that work proved lucrative, too. Between the prostitution and selling drugs, we pulled in a decent income. I distanced myself from my family as I fell right back into my old world. Each night, while I slipped into my lingerie and high heels, I convinced myself that this was just the life I was meant to live. There was no other way. Once a prostitute, always a prostitute.

My boyfriend encouraged me to go back down to Los Angeles to work for a few weeks. We both knew the johns paid well down there, and I could make some serious money in a very short time. I left for California, and while I was there, my father called me.

"I have your daughter," he said. "Your boyfriend dropped her off. Look, I know what you're doing, and I don't approve of it. I'm going to keep her with me until you get your life on track."

"Okay, that's probably best," I told him with a sigh. "Thank you for watching her."

But when I returned to Seattle, I realized I could not be away from my daughter. I called my father, but he did not answer his phone. When I still could not reach him after some time, I panicked and called the police. When they arrived, I explained the situation.

"My dad has my daughter and won't give her back. Can you help me?" I pleaded.

"Do you have the court documents stating you have full custody?" the officer asked.

"No, I've always had custody of her. But I have her birth certificate."

"I'm sorry, but there's nothing we can do without the legal documents."

The officer then informed me there was a warrant out

for my arrest for failing to pay traffic tickets. She hauled me off to jail and put me through the booking process. Once out of the holding cell and in the interrogation room, the officer who'd arrested me cuffed me to a chair.

"We're taking your children into custody," she said. "You need to get your life back on track."

I began to freak out, a huge lump forming in my throat and beads of sweat trickling down my forehead at the very thought of losing my children. "I'm really trying," I promised. "Please, give me another chance!"

The officer listed off the things I needed to do before I'd get my children back. I panicked. Though I knew my lifestyle was less than ideal, I also knew I loved my children deeply. I could not imagine my life without them. What was I going to do now?

My boyfriend got arrested a short time later for selling drugs. With my children now in foster care and him in jail, I felt completely lost and alone. I moved into a nasty hotel room on one of the worst streets in Seattle and returned to stripping at the clubs. Each day, I took a taxi to work, often stripping from 10 a.m. to 2 a.m. I snorted cocaine and drank booze all day to escape my misery. I grew extremely depressed and began experimenting with other drugs. Soon nothing, from prescription meds to meth, was off limits. The days and nights blurred together as I grew more and more numb. I continued this lifestyle for the next year.

One day, as I sat at the bar at one of the clubs, I watched two older women dancing on the two stages up

HOPE BEYOND THE STREETS

front. A couple guys sauntered in on their lunch break and took a seat.

As the women twirled around and tried to seduce them, the guys began to laugh and make fun of them. Their comments grew especially rude, and suddenly, I had an awakening.

If I don't stop what I'm doing, I'm going to be 40 years old like these women and be laughed at just like them. I will end up with nothing.

The reality hit me with such force that I felt I'd been punched in the gut. I stared at the women, their slightly aged faces covered in heavy makeup. *Please, oh please, don't let that be me. There has to be another way. I can't do this anymore.*

I got up, went back to my hotel room and called my mother. We had not talked in some time, and I knew she didn't trust me anymore. She'd even discouraged me from seeing the rest of my family because of the lifestyle I'd chosen.

"I need help," I told her desperately. "I'm in bad shape."

She helped me find a drug detox center, and I called them up. "I need help," I blurted, repeating my story.

"We happen to have a bed open," they said. "You can come in tomorrow."

My mother took me to the detox center the next day. I decided to stay away from drugs that morning but weakened and got high and drunk before she picked me up.

She tried to take me to lunch, but I refused her offer. "If I eat, I'm gonna be sick," I told her, embarrassed.

My mother began to cry. I knew I'd greatly disappointed her over the years and that she must be worried sick. I'd lost a great deal of weight, and my clothes now hung off my tiny frame. We drove in silence to the detox center, and she helped me check in.

"You need a treatment program," the woman at the center told me.

"No, I'm fine. I just need to detox," I insisted.

"No, you need treatment," she said firmly.

I agreed to enter a 30-day inpatient treatment program. After graduating, I called my Child Protective Services caseworker and told her I'd gotten clean.

"You made the right decision," she said. "Good job. Just stay on track, and you'll be able to get your kids back."

I went to an outpatient treatment program next, determined to gain custody of my kids again. One day, one of my counselors asked me how I'd gotten into drugs.

"I was forced into prostitution," I confessed. "I started using as a way to escape."

The counselor looked at me with sympathetic eyes. "I know of a lady in Vancouver who runs an organization that helps rescue girls from prostitution and sex trafficking," she said. She told me her name and added that she was a pastor's wife.

Wow! That's cool, I thought to myself. I went home and eagerly searched for the woman on Facebook. When I saw her name pop up, a spark of hope ran through me. I sent her a private message, explaining that I really wanted to talk to someone. She responded right away and asked if I could meet for coffee. I agreed to the idea.

Dr. Cyndi Romine was warm and friendly as we sat down for coffee a few days later. As we began to talk, however, I grew hesitant to share my story. "I don't want to talk about everything," I told her.

"That's okay," she replied kindly.

But 15 minutes later, I warmed up and spilled all the details, every last one. I told her how my first pimp beat me when I did not make my quotas and how I'd feared for my life. I told her how I'd been raped and pushed out of a car by strangers. I told her how I'd resorted to drugs to escape the pain. Tears filled my eyes as I recounted it all, and Dr. Romine listened like a trusted friend. She told me there was nothing I could say that would shock her — she had heard it all since beginning her work. She ran an organization, *Called to Rescue*, which helped girls like me escape a life of prostitution. Many of the girls, she explained, had stories identical to my own. They'd started off in decent homes, but one fateful night, they were snatched off the streets, and their lives had never been the same again. Dr. Romine explained the concept of brainwashing, which she referred to as "trauma bonding." Pimps used this technique to keep girls from escaping, feeding them lies that no one would ever love them after they'd been a whore on the streets.

As I mulled over her explanation, I realized that it described my relationship with each of my pimps. I'd truly believed Andre loved me, for example, convinced that no one understood me like he did. Because he did not hit me and because he treated me well and lavished me with nice things, I believed he really cared about me. I now realized I'd been brainwashed. None of them loved me — they simply used me to make money.

"The good news is, you can leave that life behind," Dr. Romine encouraged me, her eyes full of compassion. "You are valuable, and you can make a good life for yourself. I can help you get your life back on track. You were a victim of sex trafficking, just like millions of other girls around the world. This is not your fault. It's not too late for you. Are you willing to leave it all behind and move forward?"

"Yes! I'll do anything to get my kids back," I told her adamantly.

From that moment on, Dr. Cyndi Romine and I formed a special friendship. I began attending church with her regularly and enjoyed surrounding myself with positive people. Dr. Cyndi helped me take care of my outstanding warrants and helped me get my children back. Her organization also assisted me in getting a new job. After taking all the needed steps to prove that I was serious about getting my life on track, *Called to Rescue* approved me for a fully furnished reduced-rent apartment, and I moved in with my two kids.

"Thank you," I told Dr. Cyndi as I settled into my new place. "I couldn't have done all this without you." I will be forever grateful to *Called to Rescue* for helping me re-establish my life. I'd gone from a desperate, floundering girl to one who knew her purpose and value and had a clear-cut direction for the future.

My life has continued in a positive, upward direction. I've established a good relationship with my mother again, and we enjoy a friendship like we hadn't had in years. I began traveling around with Dr. Romine, doing speaking engagements with her. The more I shared my story, the more confident I grew. I eventually went on to repeat the very words Dr. Romine had encouraged me with during our first coffee meeting.

"If you want to get out, you have to first make a commitment to yourself," I've told many girls who struggled just as I had. "Don't do it for anyone else, including your kids. Do it for yourself. Everything else will follow." I hope my story can reach far and wide, impacting both people seeking to prevent sex trafficking and those who have fallen victim to it themselves.

I now recognize that because I never felt truly affirmed by my father, I had very low self-esteem. That caused me to fall in with the wrong crowd, and it was in the midst of that reckless lifestyle that I got swept into an even worse life of prostitution. Though I was a victim, I did not always understand that. I believed I was worthless, that no man would ever love me. But now, I know that was not true. With Dr. Cyndi's help and encouragement, I have come to recognize that I have value because God loves me. Slowly, I've also begun to believe that I have a beautiful future ahead of me. And I cannot wait for the next chapter of my life to begin.

CALLED TO RESCUE

❧❧❧

"Mommy, Mommy!"

My children bounded through my bedroom door and pounced on me, planting sweet kisses on my cheek as I rubbed the sleep from my eyes. I scooped them into my arms and squeezed them tightly. As the morning sun streamed through my apartment window, I savored the precious moment before our busy day began.

After another round of snuggles and kisses, the children pattered out of the room, and I slid out of bed to get dressed for work. As I glanced around my apartment, a contented smile reached the corner of my mouth. Now 27, I am a thriving mother of two. I hold a steady job and live a happy life. My road has been long and hard, but I am grateful to be alive. I'm also grateful to *Called to Rescue* for helping me get my life back on track. With their encouragement, I've learned to value myself and not define myself by the past.

"Come on, kids!" I called out. "Time to go!"

As their little faces popped around the corner, I couldn't help but smile again.

Thank you, God, for these children. I'll never take a minute with them for granted.

Thank you for fresh starts. I'm never going back to my old life. You have rescued me.

There is hope beyond the streets.

One of the girls I rescued was 30 years old. We took her off the street and went to the nearest restaurant and fed her. As we talked, I asked her if she had any children. She said yes. Her son was 16 months old. I asked where he was, and she informed me that he was at home with her mother and husband.

Her mother and husband had sent her out to make the equivalent of $6.00. She was told not to come home until she had that amount. We gave her the $6.00 and sent her home.

What did that give her? One night off the street. One night she might not be beaten. One night of peace in her heart that she would not have to "perform."

One night!

THE COURAGE TO FIND FREEDOM
THE STORY OF ROSE
LOCATION: HONG KONG
WRITTEN BY KAREN KOCZWARA

The Philippines, home to 97 million people, including me and my family. With a staggering poverty level, even those with the best education struggle to survive. My husband, like many men, worked as a teacher but made very little money. We struggled to find work and constantly scrambled for ways to feed our children. We were not alone. Every family I knew was striving, pulling, scrimping and saving. With so much competition, our plight became especially difficult. The equation was simple — too many people and not enough jobs. The result was a daily battle to make ends meet.

It's a desperate life, watching your children starve. I wept silently many nights, knowing my children had not had enough to eat that day. As I heard their stomachs growl and watched their wide, hopeful eyes, my heart broke. I felt helpless. I could only pray that tomorrow might bring something different — some opportunity to change our fate and reverse the depressing cycle.

One day, I heard rumors on the streets. Several men were hiring for a large company in Hong Kong. They were looking for women to fill a variety of jobs depending on their skills. Women of all ages were moving to another country to work as a nanny, domestic worker, office worker, model, singer or even an actress.

The offer seemed too good to be true, but the possibility too good to pass up. I could send money home to my family. My husband and I talked it over. We loved each other so much, and the thought of living in separate countries seemed heartbreaking. As I gazed at my children, sleeping near me, I ached at the thought of not seeing them. But what if a temporary sacrifice could turn our lives around?

The money I could make might mean we'd never go hungry again. Better yet, perhaps there would be other luxuries we'd never dreamed of before — new clothes, a new house, money for college someday. We had to give it a try.

I arrived at an agency office in Manila. Everyone was so professional and kind. The receptionist welcomed me and offered me a seat as I waited for the recruiter. Sitting across from her, I grew both hopeful and nervous. Her hair was done just so, her business attire obviously brand-new, clean, pressed and perfect. I looked down at my own threadbare skirt and tried to cover the stains with my hands. Her nails were freshly manicured and clacked away on her keyboard. I looked down at my own calloused hands, embarrassed. I longed to have soft, manicured hands. With every click of her beautiful red fingertips, I imagined the meals and clothes my children would have. Her children surely never went hungry.

"Rose?" The receptionist called me out of my reverie, me gazing at my hands, imagining their soft, manicured future. "The recruiter will see you now."

The receptionist showed me to a small room and sat me down with a pile of papers. She instructed me that they needed all this information to find the appropriate placement for me, and if I needed any assistance, the recruiter would help me fill it out.

"Complete as much of the paperwork as you can. The recruiter will be with you in just a minute," she said on her way out.

I barely heard a word she said as I stared at the giant stack of forms. *What sort of questions are they going to ask? Is this some sort of test? What if I don't pass?* My pulse quickened as the thoughts raced through my mind. But I then thought of my family. My hope of obtaining a job in my country was quickly waning. The reluctance I felt at leaving my family was now overshadowed by desperation. I needed this job. I had to get it. Isn't this exactly what I had been praying for?

I gripped my pencil and did my best to fill in the blanks. The forms required me to provide an extensive medical history and personal background, including any diseases I'd had or still suffered from. It also asked me to include my family history, where I had lived, any training and education.

The paperwork described several of the job opportunities and requirements. I scanned them, my heart sinking as I realized I would not be eligible for several of them because of my age. I was also married, which wasn't desirable for the position of a nanny or domestic worker. My chances were getting slimmer by the minute.

The recruiter knocked quietly before he entered. I gulped as I stood, wishing I could hide my overworked hands and worn clothes. Well-educated, well-dressed and well-built, he looked even more intimidating than the receptionist. His hair, with a bit of silver peeking in at his temples, was freshly cut, his hands as soft and well cared for as the receptionist's. He was obviously born and raised in Hong Kong. As we greeted one another, I couldn't help but guess the small fortune he must have spent on his appearance. Could this man help me feed my children? He certainly looked like he could.

THE COURAGE TO FIND FREEDOM

"Well, it looks like you got a lot done while you were waiting!" he said with a smile as he sat and skimmed through my paperwork.

I tried to smile back, but my lips stuck together, my mouth dry from my nervousness. I managed a small smile as I wiped my palms on my skirt, trying to disguise my fear.

"I see you got to the job descriptions. Do any of these positions look particularly interesting to you?"

"Well, I had hoped for a position as a nanny or domestic worker. But I am married and older than the preferred age for a nanny," I said sheepishly.

"Oh, don't worry about all that!" he returned with a warm chuckle. "That's just a guideline. I can see from your skill at filling out these forms and the answers you provided that you would do extremely well in either of those positions. You aren't too much older than the age listed, and your marriage really isn't an issue since your husband won't be living in Hong Kong with you. If we find a suitable placement, we can provide you with the appropriate documents and just adjust your age and marital status."

Adjust my age and marital status? I gulped again and shifted my gaze downward. I didn't want to lie. If my future employers discovered the truth about me, they might fire me immediately, and all my hopes and dreams would be shattered.

"Really, Rose, don't worry." He gently placed his hand on mine, obviously aware of my nervousness. "I can tell you are very eager, and I am just as dedicated to finding you a job. I will do everything I can to help you help your family."

We continued the interview, and he kindly assisted me with the completion of the forms. He was extremely professional, yet so warm and gracious.

"There are many jobs you are qualified for," he assured me repeatedly. "You might even find work as a model."

I giggled with embarrassment, staring once again at my calloused hands and old clothes. *Me, a model?* That seemed a bit far-fetched. "I don't know about that," I stammered.

"We place women like you as models all the time," he continued. "I see it all the time. There is something shiny beneath your surface, Rose, and we just have to bring that out. With some makeup, new clothes and a nice haircut, we could have you on the cover of a magazine in no time."

That all sounded a bit extravagant to me. I would be just as happy working as a nanny and sending paychecks home to my family. The recruiter took a couple of Polaroid pictures of me to attach to the paperwork.

After our interview, he escorted me to the front door, passing his lovely receptionist once again. This time, I envisioned myself in her place. My hair done just so, nails perfect, brand-new clothes. And children at home with full bellies and brand-new clothes of their own.

"I'll text you as soon as your paperwork is processed, but I must warn you that it can take quite some time," the recruiter told me as we parted ways. "Just be patient."

THE COURAGE TO FIND FREEDOM

"Thank you so much for all your help. I'll be looking for your text," I told him gratefully.

I hurried home, eager to tell my husband how the interview had gone. From the recruiter's demeanor, I felt sure I would get one of the positions available. I was thrilled for this change in our family's fate, yet heartbroken at the prospect of leaving my home, husband and children.

What would it be like to start a new life all alone in a foreign country? The idea was daunting yet exciting. How long would it take to process the paperwork before I departed for Hong Kong? Days, weeks? How long did I have with my little ones?

I picked up the pace, even more anxious to hug them, knowing how few hugs I had left.

☙ ☙ ☙

It took nearly 30 days to process my paperwork. My husband and I lost hope a number of times, thinking I had been forgotten or rejected somewhere along the line. When I got the text from the recruiter that my application had been accepted, my heart surged with hope.

"It's really happening! They accepted me!" I cried to my husband, happy tears pricking my eyes.

I met the recruiter at his office the next day.

"Rose! I'm so happy to see you," he greeted me warmly with a big smile as he ushered me into his office. "I told you, didn't I? You got a job in Hong Kong!"

"Yes, thank you so much. I'm so excited," I told him eagerly.

"We still need to get you the proper documentation. We'll reduce your age and list your marital status as 'single.' This will cost some money, but the good news is, there is a modeling job waiting for you in Hong Kong if you still want it." His eyes met mine as he enunciated every word. "This job will pay far more than any nanny position ever will."

A lump formed in my throat again at the idea of misrepresenting myself. *It must be done,* I convinced myself. *I cannot say no when I've come this close.*

"We'll need to have you complete your medical exam today before you leave, so I can begin working on your visa and other paperwork. Your travel expenses to Hong Kong will be about $1,200, plus the additional cost of your adjusted documentation, which means you will owe —"

"Oh," I interrupted. "That's a lot of money. I … I don't know …"

"Rose, you really need to stop worrying so much!" he chided me with a smile. "We are sending you to Hong Kong for a lucrative career. If you don't have the money right now, it will just come out of your paycheck until the debt is paid. With your new salary, you'll pay that off in no time!"

I sighed with relief, a huge smile spread across my face, and for the first time since entertaining the idea of this new life, my entire body relaxed. *This is really happening! I'm going to be a model, of all things! And in the city of*

THE COURAGE TO FIND FREEDOM

Hong Kong, of all places! My family will be safe and healthy. We will no longer need to worry where our next meal will come from. My dreams will come true at last.

☙☙☙

I completed the medical exam in a back room at the recruiter's office. A doctor came in and examined every inch of my body. He also performed a full pelvic exam. I cringed and winced with humiliation as the doctor prodded and poked. The recruiter had assured me that it was standard procedure for those wishing to live and work in Hong Kong. They didn't want any strange diseases being brought into their country. When the exam was complete, the recruiter told me to hurry home and pack my bags. I would be leaving that night for Hong Kong.

Tonight? But that's so soon! I hadn't prepared myself for such a swift departure. But the sooner I left, the sooner my children would eat a good meal, and that was an encouraging thought.

I hurried home and said my goodbyes. I didn't have much to bring with me, just a small backpack with my meager clothing and toiletries. My husband thrust a picture of our family in my hand as he pulled me close. "I love you," he whispered, his voice breaking. We held each other in a long embrace, both afraid to let go, afraid of the flood of tears that might come if we pulled apart.

My children stood close by, my tiny son struggling against his sister's arm around his shoulder, unaware of why this moment was so solemn. He grew impatient, wanting to return to his playtime. I crouched down and gave him a hug, reluctant to let go, but also aware of his innocence, his complete lack of understanding of the situation. I kissed him on the cheek and released him to resume his toddler adventures. I then turned to my daughter, who suddenly looked so grown up at 5 years old. "It's okay, Mama, don't cry," she comforted me sweetly as tears filled my eyes. "I'll be a good girl and work hard for Daddy. I'll look after Brother."

I held her tightly and struggled to keep the tears back. I didn't want her to see me cry. *If our plan works, little one, your days of hard work are over,* I thought, my heart breaking for all of us.

"I'll be home very soon," I assured her, trying to make myself believe it. With the amount of money I was promised as a model, I would surely be able to afford trips home to visit, wouldn't I? And perhaps we could save enough that this life of separation would only be temporary.

With that thought, I cleared my throat and wiped my tears as we ended our embrace. I gave her one final kiss on the forehead, and my husband a final quick peck, wanting to leave before another flood of tears came. I slung my small bag over my shoulder and headed for Hong Kong, hoping all our dreams and plans would soon become reality.

ೞೞೞ

THE COURAGE TO FIND FREEDOM

Once I arrived in Hong Kong, I found myself in the middle of a large, beautiful airport. Bustling passengers, bright lights and loud noises greeted me as I stepped off the plane. I felt very tired, lost, bewildered and overwhelmed from the flight and emotionally exhausted from leaving my family and home. I had stared out the airplane window as the rice paddies drifted away, watching every person, every place I had ever known shrink into the distance. Now my feet were firmly planted in Hong Kong, and a new, very different life was about to begin.

I frantically glanced around the airport terminal, searching for the person from the agency holding a sign bearing my name. I spotted a young man peeking through the sea of passengers; he was bearing a cardboard sign with the name "Rose" scrawled on it.

I gingerly pushed my way through the crowd to reach him. "Hi, I'm Rose. Are you from the modeling agency?"

I assumed he would be much like the recruiter and the receptionist. I had grown accustomed to their warmth and easy smiles. But something about his demeanor seemed different.

"Yep. Gimme your passport, all your IDs and your return ticket," he demanded, holding out his hand.

I took a step back, suddenly reluctant as he glared at me coldly. *Why is he snapping at me?*

"Okay, just a moment …" I fumbled for my documents.

"Come on! Hand 'em over. We don't have all day!

CALLED TO RESCUE

How do you expect to make any money if you can't follow simple instructions?" he pressed, already quite frustrated. He now seemed distracted, as though he was looking right through me instead of at me.

I quickly handed over everything he asked for, nervous that I might still lose this opportunity to save my family. *I'll be the hardest worker they've ever seen,* I decided, suddenly determined. *I'll need to remember to follow directions as soon as they are given. This is a different world after all. I don't want my inexperience to get me in trouble.* I hurried after him out of the airport into the heart of the city.

Welcome to Hong Kong, Rose. You're not a farm girl anymore.

❦❦❦

There is no city on earth like Hong Kong. Hundreds of high-rise buildings overlook the beautiful Victoria Harbor, offering some of the most stunning views in the world from their top floors. Temples, posh shopping malls, markets and skyscrapers sit side by side on the tiny peninsula that seven million people call home. From morning until night, the city bustles with business and tourism, never sleeping even after the sun goes down. Known as a shopper's paradise, visitors from all over the world flock to Hong Kong every year to enjoy the glitz and glamour. Tourists can take a tram to the top of the mountain to experience breathtaking island views or enjoy

THE COURAGE TO FIND FREEDOM

the dazzling Symphony of Lights laser and fireworks show over the harbor at night. With its mild tropical winters, Hong Kong's weather attracts people looking to escape the harsh, frigid months. From the top looking down, Hong Kong is a beacon of beauty, life and power. But on the streets, life is not so glamorous.

Thousands of tourists and locals line the narrow streets of Hong Kong every day. People walk hurriedly down the city streets, like sardines jammed into the crowded sidewalks. Little old women sit on the corners playing mahjong, selling their homemade goods or cooking in open cauldrons. Open-air markets offer everything from natural medicines in baskets to cups of fish soup. People huddle under restaurant tents, hoping to escape the sweltering summer sun. Air conditioners from apartment buildings drip water on people's heads as they shuffle by. Locals gamble in the streets, and pornography is openly displayed on every corner. The humidity often grows so thick that the air becomes sticky and foggy, making it difficult to breathe amidst the massive crowds. This is the world I was ushered into, and I hadn't a clue what lay ahead.

☙☙☙

The driver stopped the car on a busy street and barked at me to get out. We paced the streets, and I took in the smells, the sounds and the sights. The muggy air grew stifling as throngs of people brushed up against me on the sidewalks. A woman selling baskets cooked something on an open cauldron as we walked by. I stopped to peak in the cauldron and discovered just what she had brewing — snakes! I watched in awe as she deftly pulled the skin off the snake with one hand and gutted the creature with a pair of pliers in one motion. Right there on the street!

The driver barked at me again. I was walking too slowly. We would be late. I hurried past the woman and her cauldron and forced myself to keep up. There would be plenty of time to explore all of Hong Kong. Right now, I needed to get to work.

We made our way toward what I would later come to know as the Wan Chai area, which has one of the most prominent "red light" districts in the city. I glanced around and saw young girls pacing the streets, puffing on cigarettes as they lingered outside the brightly lit nightclubs. Like me, most were young Filipino women, but instead of drab dresses they wore carefully applied makeup, bikini tops, short miniskirts and thigh-high black boots. The girls looked like they were in their early 20s, though some seemed much older, the faint lines on their faces telling a sad story of a life of emptiness and pain.

I gripped my bag close to my chest as we shuffled past the girls. I tried my best not to stare, but I couldn't help wondering why we were here. How had these girls — who looked like my friends from back home — ended up lined up on this filthy boulevard, dressed in this way, selling themselves in this manner? I would soon find out.

The driver ushered me past the girls standing on the

stoop of one of the clubs and inside the darkened doorway. I clutched my bag even tighter, frightened of my surroundings. He prodded me forward and then shoved me into a back room where an older woman sat waiting.

"Take off your clothes. Put this on," she instructed abruptly, tossing me some new clothes.

I stared at her, confused. "Right now?" I stammered.

The woman glared at me disdainfully. "I know your story. Seen a hundred of you. You have a debt to pay back, and you're going to pay it back by sleeping with men."

I glanced at the clothes in my hand — the very sort of clothes I'd just seen the young Filipino girls wearing outside. *Is she serious? There must be some mistake. The recruiter told me I'd become a model!* I glanced frantically around the dark room, wondering if I might be able to run away. But I didn't know where I'd go. I didn't know my way around this giant city. I began to perspire as I realized that I had been tricked. I had nothing on me and no way to get home. No plane ticket, no passport, no ID. I was stranded, at this strange woman's mercy.

My hands trembled as I clutched my bag possessively. Before I could open my mouth to protest, the cruel woman ripped my bag out of my hands and thrust my new "uniform" at me once again. "Did you hear what I said? Or should I have one of my boys come beat some sense into you? You have nothing. You have no one. And you owe us a great deal of money. If you don't sleep with the men you saw outside, we will go get your husband, your children. Someone will work to pay what you owe!"

The mention of my family jolted me into motion. I had come here to save them. If I couldn't send them any money, at least I could keep them safe from more harm. I slipped off my clothes and pulled on my new work attire, sickened by what was happening. *I didn't sign up for this!*

The woman yanked me aside and began to apply my makeup. As she swept the brushes over my face, I held still, afraid to further upset her. I peeked in the mirror before me and was shocked at the transformation. *This is quite an ordeal! I've never looked like this before in my life!*

"You need to do this yourself from now on," she told me. "The more beautiful you look, the more men you'll get, and the more money you make, the faster you'll pay off your debt. That's what you want, isn't it?"

I nodded numbly in agreement.

When she was done, she stepped back and let me fully inspect myself in the mirror. *I'm so beautiful! I don't look at all like the girl who stepped on that plane yesterday!* I knew that I would gain quite a bit of attention from the eager customers outside. My heart began to race in fear at the thought of what they would want to do to me, what they would be purchasing me for.

The woman saw my reluctance returning and swiftly slapped me across the face. "Think of your family! That's what your children have in store if you don't pay your debt. Now go!" She shoved me out the door and onto the street.

I stepped outside, teetering in my new high heels as

THE COURAGE TO FIND FREEDOM

the dim lights of the club flickered above. I had never worn heels this high in my life. I glanced around and saw several girls trying to lure men their way. Several men eyed me with looks of lust and longing, and a few began to approach me. My stomach lurched at the idea of touching them, but my cheek still stung from the woman's assault. I thought again of my children and the debt I must pay back. With as much courage as I could muster, I attempted a sultry smile and led a gentleman back into the club. The old woman smiled at me, obviously pleased at how quickly I'd returned with a customer, and motioned to a back room. *Please, let this be quick,* I prayed, closing my eyes for a moment. *Let this nightmare all be over soon so I can go back home.*

But that night was just the beginning of the nightmare. I would not go home anytime soon. Instead, I'd be sucked into a life I'd never known existed, and I would find it nearly impossible to escape.

☙☙☙

I met Dr. Cyndi in 1992. She was living in Hong Kong, and we were introduced by an elderly Filipino woman I had known for quite some time. I was in my mid-30s, having lived and worked in Hong Kong for nearly a decade. Gone was the timid and demure girl fresh off the plane. I carried an air of authority in my speech and demeanor. I dressed impeccably in designer clothes and wore sparkling, carefully applied makeup.

CALLED TO RESCUE

Dr. Cyndi and I developed a friendship. She told me about her passion to help rescue young women from sex trafficking. I had never heard my work referred to in such terms. We had coffee and lunches, and during our visits, I shared only certain details of my life with her, the magnitude of my influence. I had become a madam who ran a group of girls and operated several prominent nightclubs in the city, primarily catering to British, Chinese and Japanese men. I remained vague about my past, not wanting to remember those horrible early days, not wanting to fully disclose who I had once been and what I had now become.

"Rose. I have to ask. You are so poised! It's hard for me to understand how a woman like you fell into the world of prostitution." Dr. Cyndi's eyes were kind and genuinely inquisitive as she spoke.

"It is a hard life. We do what we need to do," I told her slowly. I briefly explained how so many of us fell into this life, how we were sucked in and trapped with no hope of escape. "Not all the women the agency brings over end up in my shoes," I added. I went on to describe some of the other girls' plights.

Some girls land legitimate jobs as domestic workers, but their lives are far from glamorous. To ensure their husbands do not fall in love with the new nanny or maid, the female employers force the girls into drab, baggy attire. Many are sexually, emotionally and physically abused. Some are not even offered a bed and must sleep on the hard kitchen floor at night. Most work long, laborious days with only one day off a week. Some work months straight without a break. They quickly realize the life they hoped to have is not what they imagined. But they cannot speak up or talk back to their employer because they have no other options. Their passports are gone. They are in debt. They have no way to get home and are far too embarrassed to tell their families about their predicament. They are stuck in a bustling city where no one knows their name or cares about their needs. They are frightened and helpless. They are trapped.

Afraid, vulnerable and alone in a foreign country, stripped of all their possessions, the girls have no choice but to obey. The aspiring model, like me, discovers there is no modeling agency waiting for her — there will be no magazine shoot. The hopeful singer learns that there is no promising recording contract in her future. The girl who dreams of becoming an actress soon realizes that she'll never grace the big screen. They have been lied to and tricked. They are stranded, forced into a life of prostitution on the streets of Hong Kong. Required to sleep with hundreds of strange men in exchange for money. They must trade in their souls and give up their dreams. Many never escape or see their families again.

Dr. Cyndi was eager to meet as many of these girls as she could, and I introduced her to many of them during her stay. On Sundays, many Filipino workers took advantage of their only day off and headed to the bustling Central Park. This was their "Cinderella" day, when they could shed their drab working clothes and wear beautiful dresses for a few precious hours. They enjoyed eating their own ethnic foods, shopping and mingling with others who spoke their own language. For just a little while, they could pretend they were back in their home country — safe, happy and free. But when the clock struck midnight, they were forced to return to work, leaving the fancy shoes behind.

"I want to help," Dr. Cyndi told me. "My work has brought me here because I want to rescue these girls out of this lifestyle. I can help them find new jobs. There are choices out there."

Dr. Cyndi said they deserved a better life. But I knew that, like me, they had stopped dreaming about one long ago. For the first time in a very long while, however, I felt something — hope. I wondered if Dr. Cyndi might be right. Perhaps there was another way.

☙☙☙

"I do not want to be in this business anymore," I confessed to Dr. Cyndi one night. "I need your help."

"That's what I'm here for," Dr. Cyndi assured me kindly.

She looked into my eyes. I felt she could see right through me, see the hundreds of stories, thousands of men. I was hiding behind them. Though perfectly put together on the outside, I was crumbling inside. I wanted out. Unfortunately, it was not that simple. I made a great deal of money doing what I did. If I left the lifestyle

THE COURAGE TO FIND FREEDOM

behind, I'd risk losing everything. I could wind up destitute and go right back on the streets where I began.

But Dr. Cyndi had helped me believe in another way. Her stories had shown me I did not have to spend the rest of my days in the midst of prostitution. Dr. Cyndi had saved many other girls and continued to convince me that through *Called to Rescue*, a new lifestyle was possible.

I didn't just want to save myself. There were many girls who worked for me. Many, I knew, had similar stories to my own. They had left behind husbands and children long ago, afraid they'd never see them again. I had seen their hollow eyes and sad smiles, and I knew they'd given up on a better life. Little girls dream of being princesses in shiny ball gowns, not walking the streets in high-heeled boots and miniskirts. Even if I could not get out, I at least wanted to help these girls.

With Dr. Cyndi's help, I could give these girls hope again and set them free.

❧❧❧

Dr. Cyndi didn't waste any time. We met the girls in restaurants, where Dr. Cyndi shared how they could escape and find a new life. It wasn't hard to convince most of them, especially hearing the hope in Dr. Cyndi's voice, her compassion and understanding and willingness to partner with them in complete rehabilitation. The girls listened intently, bobbing their heads up and down as Dr. Cyndi spoke.

CALLED TO RESCUE

"Will you trust me and come with me?" Dr. Cyndi asked them.

They nodded, and I breathed a deep sigh of relief. Their hands, wrung together in apprehension just moments before, now relaxed, and I saw in their faces a sense of excitement. They were about to be free. They would not spend one more night standing on the dark, dirty streets outside the clubs, trying to seduce men with their lipsticked smiles. They would be free to live a normal life again, one where people knew them by their real names. They were going to be okay.

As I saw the influence Dr. Cyndi had on these girls, I began to mull over the idea of trying something greater. It would require some risk, but it was a risk I was willing to take.

"I want you to go to one of my clubs and talk to my girls," I told Dr. Cyndi one night, looking her square in the eye.

Dr. Cyndi, always up for anything, took a deep breath. "Okay. Just tell me what to do."

❧❧❧

The next afternoon, I met Dr. Cyndi as she stepped off the elevator into my ninth-floor club, surrounded by several well-dressed men. She was clad in a pretty sundress and clearly stood out among my patrons.

"Boy, do I have a surprise for those guys!" she whispered to me as I led her through the huge doors into my club. She glanced around, obviously surprised by the luxuriousness of the place. Booths lined the outside of the room, complete with lush deep maroon and red upholstery. A bar with drinks and food sat in the corner. Large windows were completely covered, keeping the late-afternoon sunlight from streaming through. Men of all ethnicities squeezed into the booths, eating and sipping their drinks. Disco lights flashed, projecting colorful patterns on the walls and floor. Loud music thumped as girls danced around the large stage at the center of the room, clad in miniskirts, high heels and expensive jewelry.

I glanced at several of their faces, struck as I often was by their beauty beneath the glitter and makeup. As they danced, my heart went out to them. The woman standing next to me was about to change their fates. I would no longer be part of their downfall. I had found them a savior. "You are going to be the next one on the stage," I whispered to Dr. Cyndi.

"Give me a moment," she replied, slipping to the restroom to collect her thoughts. As Dr. Cyndi prepared for her debut, I surveyed the room, this business I had built. How had this happened? How had I become an employer of young women trapped in prostitution just as I had been? I was ashamed of my participation in this industry. Inviting Dr. Cyndi to speak to them, to save them, made me extremely proud. I was finally doing something good, something that didn't make me ashamed.

I blinked back tears as Dr. Cyndi emerged from the bathroom. We nodded at one another, and she climbed

CALLED TO RESCUE

onto the stage, cleared her throat and glanced out into the crowd. The men stared back at her, confused by the sudden change of tone. I said a silent prayer for my friend on stage, just as she began to speak. The music stopped, the lights stopped flashing and the disco balls were suddenly stilled.

"Today is a new day, ladies. You can leave here with me now, and you will find the destiny God has for you."

She grew bolder as she continued to speak, her voice now strong and bold as it echoed across the room. She gave the speech I'd heard her give many times before, when we met with girls individually, but this time she had a much larger audience. These men had paid top dollar to be seduced. They might be disappointed — angry even. They could turn on both of us violently.

She promised she would help them find new jobs in Hong Kong or help them get home. She explained that she had the legal connections to help rescue them from the lifestyle they'd been sucked into. She spoke to the men as well, stressing that they did not need to try to find fulfillment in nightclubs. This seemed particularly brave to me, speaking directly to the customers.

"I am leaving this place now, and so can you. Get your belongings, ladies, and come with Rose and me now." She then calmly walked off the stage.

Will they go with her? Or is she about to be attacked? I suddenly feared for my friend's life, realizing I may have handed her over to an angry mob of insulted Hong Kong johns.

THE COURAGE TO FIND FREEDOM

To my shock, most of the girls grabbed their purses and followed her. The music restarted, blaring in the background as they walked right past those heavy doors. The clicking of their high heels echoed as they headed for the elevator. It was the exodus I had hoped for. I stood there surveying the scene, the dumbfounded faces of the businessmen around me. I felt a tear run down my cheek. *She did it. We did it. Go, girls. Go and be free.*

༶༶༶

We stood outside the tall building, the sun just setting over the harbor as we composed ourselves. The girls huddled together, still clutching their purses. My heart still thumped in my chest as I replayed the whirlwind of events in my mind. *We really did it! We just walked them out of that club!*

People marched by, heading home for dinner after a long day's work. Tourists stopped to take photos of the scenery, and hawkers barked to the crowd, selling their wares to the passersby. To them, it was just another ordinary day in the bustling city of Hong Kong. But to us, it was the first day of the rest of our lives. What had just taken place inside that club was nothing less than extraordinary. And I owed it all to Dr. Cyndi.

"I could not have done that without you," I gushed gratefully.

"Now the hard part begins." She winked as she hugged me, celebrating our success. I wasn't exactly sure what the next steps entailed, but something very important had been accomplished. The girls had willingly come with us. They had hope. Dr. Cyndi had given them courage.

I was thrilled that we'd saved so many of the girls. Over a two-week period, we had rescued around 50 of my girls from prostitution. We cried tears of joy, rejoicing together that our mission had been a success.

As happy as I was to have completed the rescue, I was also faced with a startling reality — I was now out of a job.

❧❧❧

The day after the rescue, I went to Dr. Cyndi in tears. Hearing the stories of so many of the women I employed struck something deep within me, a deep shame I had been harboring for more than a decade.

"I can never go home to my country!" I cried. "My husband and children know what I've done, and they will never forgive me!"

Though I'd successfully run one of the most prestigious clubs in the city, I now found myself unemployed. I stood before Dr. Cyndi, a well-dressed yet broken woman, torn and afraid. I had heard it from my employers over and over, even after I had worked so long and so hard that my debt must have been paid off. "You're a whore. You'll never be anything but a whore. How many men have you slept with? Hundreds? Thousands? Your husband would be disgusted at the sight of you. Your children corrupted by your filthy life. They know what you have been up to, the life that you lead. They will never forgive, never accept you. You're just a whore."

Perhaps that's why I became a madam, rising in the ranks slowly but surely. I grew tired of sleeping with men, but what other life could I live? Who would employ me in any respectable profession? How would I ever get out?

Now I stood at a crossroads. My wildest dreams were finally coming true. I could finally be free of this life. With Dr. Cyndi's encouragement, I had discovered my voice. I'd finally broken free from a life that had trapped me for years, and I now had the chance to go home. But could I face my family again? The tears of shame and fear overwhelmed me once again.

Dr. Cyndi reminded me of what we'd told the girls. They were not alone. God had another plan. This was not the end, but the beginning of a beautiful life.

"I will go home, Mommy," I decided, using my term of endearment for Dr. Cyndi. "I have no future here in Hong Kong." Dr. Cyndi's words strengthened me. I was terribly afraid, but her belief in me bolstered my confidence.

"You will be okay," she told me. She made me feel brave.

❧❧❧

We then began discussing our next steps. We took the girls to lunch and helped them sort out their problems. Each one shared a different heart-wrenching story. Most had families back home who did not know what they'd been doing. Some were married with children. Many wanted to return to their native land but felt trapped in Hong Kong. Though they should have made good money dancing in my club, they never received a dime of it. As I stared into their frightened faces, I saw myself in them, and my heart began to break. *What sort of life have we created for them? Surely, this was never how things were meant to be. Yes, we are all victims in our own ways, but this is not the end for us now. Thanks to Dr. Cyndi and Called to Rescue, we know there is another way.*

Before I left, Dr. Cyndi and I helped the girls get on their way. The biggest issue was, of course, money. Each of these women was out of a job, and they certainly couldn't remain unemployed. Poverty and starvation would lure them right back into the sex industry.

Dr. Cyndi and *Called to Rescue* worked hard to obtain jobs for a majority of the girls, and she used her many connections to take care of other legal matters, such as work visas, etc. This was a huge undertaking, finding jobs for so many women, but Dr. Cyndi is tenacious, and her team at *Called to Rescue* is tireless. They labored, with great love and compassion, to keep the girls' hopes up during the process. And, one by one, they placed each former prostitute into a new life.

I didn't have Dr. Cyndi's many connections, but I did what I could. I helped the girls sell their fancy jewelry and Rolex watches to pay for one-way plane tickets home, and what they couldn't cover, I paid for out of my own pocket. I prayed they would find acceptance and happiness when they returned to their home country. I prayed I would find the same. It had taken a great deal of courage for them to walk out of that club and to trust their lives to a complete stranger, but Dr. Cyndi helped all of us believe we would find a brighter future. And she made that future a reality, for each and every one of us.

※ ※ ※

Two years later, I was back home in the Philippines, reunited with my husband and children, living the life Dr. Cyndi had described. A life of hope and love and acceptance, reunited with my loved ones, forgiven and accepted and healed. One day, I was riding in our car with my husband, and as I passed a large, prestigious hotel, I saw her. I screamed so loudly, the driver screeched to a halt. I jumped out of the car and ran toward her, throwing myself into her arms. I began kissing her neck and crying hysterically. I couldn't believe my eyes! It was really her!

"Dr. Cyndi, I have not seen you in so long!" I exclaimed through tears. Clad in a pair of simple jeans, my layers of makeup and glitter now gone, I must have looked like a completely different person, not at all the exquisitely dressed madam she'd met in Hong Kong.

"Rose, it's so great to see you!" She pulled me back into her arms, and we cried and hugged for a long time.

"It's a miracle!" I gushed. I began to tell her everything. "My family has taken me back! We just finished having Christmas together!"

CALLED TO RESCUE

"Oh, Rose, that's wonderful!" Tears of joy now spilled down her cheeks. God had completely restored my life, giving me a second chance in my home country where I belonged. And here was the woman to whom I owed everything. My rescuer, here in the flesh.

≈≈≈

I bounce my granddaughter on my knee, laughing at her older brother's attempts to make her smile. He doesn't like it when his baby sister cries. As I glance out the window of the church, my heart surges with happiness. Never in a million years did I imagine I could be a pastor. But I am now leading a church on this gorgeous island, ministering to people in the heart of this notorious party city.

Known around the world for its pristine white sandy beaches, it is one of the most popular party destinations in the Philippines. An entire mile of nightclubs, restaurants and other tourist attractions line these postcard-worthy beaches. Like Hong Kong, it dazzles from a distance. But darkness lies beneath the bright lights, sucking people into a life of drugs, alcohol and destruction. I know that darkness, because I lived in it for many years. But I am free now, and I want to reach others with the good news of hope.

"You silly little girl!" I nuzzle my granddaughter's chubby cheeks, and again, I am filled with joy. These days, there is much to celebrate. Thanks to Dr. Cyndi and

THE COURAGE TO FIND FREEDOM

Called to Rescue, I no longer hide behind rouge, lipstick and fancy clothes. I am happy to return to simple ways and even happier to be with my family. There was a time when I never thought I'd see them again, but God has restored our relationships, and we are now as tight-knit as ever.

Playing with my grandchildren, I can't help but think of the last time I saw my rescuer. While Dr. Cyndi was speaking at a large conference on the topic of sex trafficking, someone notified her that I was at the meeting. I burst through the door and into the room, and we reunited with happy tears. When I told her I was now pastoring a church, I thought she might fall out of her chair. Dr. Cyndi told me she'd never seen such a picture of restoration before in her life. I know she continues to do great things with *Called to Rescue*. Hugging my grandbaby, I prayed for Dr. Cyndi just then.

I shudder thinking what my life might have been like if I had stayed in Hong Kong running that club. From the outside, I had all the wealth one could imagine. But no one on the outside knew the pain I'd endured — the many nights I'd cried myself to sleep, lonely and afraid. As I play with my beautiful grandchildren, I laugh in spite of myself. Gone is my elaborate makeup and fancy clothes. My closet might be bare, but my heart is full. *Thank you, Dr. Cyndi,* I whisper often. *Thank you.*

Every child on the street is in danger. No matter the city or part of the world, any child on the street can be taken, trafficked, victimized and exploited.

Ignorance is not bliss, it is ignorance. And pretending that the atrocities in this world do not exist is just pretending. It is certainly not reality.

– Dr. Cyndi Romine

ALL'S WELL THAT ENDS WELL
THE STORY OF LILY
LOCATION: THE PHILIPPINES
WRITTEN BY DOUGLAS ABBOTT

I was having the best dream I could remember in ages. In the dream, it was nighttime. I was sitting in my bedroom wearing a fancy nightgown, waiting for the next text I would receive from my boyfriend. He wrote me the sweetest things, in my dream. Hopes of our life together when we were old enough to get married. Compliments and kind words about how beautiful he thought I was and how lucky he was to be with me. I lay back in my large fluffy bed, covered in satin sheets, and memorized every word of every text, drinking in his love and affection.

My eyes were closed. I was listening to our housekeeper, Maggie, who was in the spare room playing her guitar, as she always did at bedtime. Her fingers *plucked the strings skillfully. The house was filled with its ethereal sounds. As I listened, I thought I heard my boyfriend sneaking in my room through the window. I could hear the noise of the window frame scraping as it came up. Silly boy, always trying to surprise me. I laughed as I heard the thumping of his shoes coming up over the windowsill. Then he was in the room. I heard him knocking items off the nightstand. Why would he be hurrying? His footsteps sounded wrong —*

I opened my eyes just in time to see a masked man reach across my bed and put his hand on my mouth. I screamed almost soundlessly. Before I could wriggle out from under him, he sat on my legs and grabbed the front of my nightgown. I couldn't move.

"Keep quiet!" he growled. He drew a revolver out of his jacket pocket and put the barrel of the gun right between my eyes.

"If you make another sound, I'm going to kill you. Then I'm going to kill everyone else in the house. Keep quiet, and do what I say."

I was too scared to resist.

The gunman was gloved and wore dark pants and a matching jacket. He put the gun back into his jacket pocket and pulled me up to a sitting position in the bed. He pulled a roll of tape out of his other jacket pocket, put a gloved finger to his lips and began peeling a strip of tape off the roll, which he placed over my mouth.

"Put your shoes on," he told me.

ALL'S WELL THAT ENDS WELL

After I had slipped my tennis shoes on, he pulled me to my feet, led me toward the door and pushed me into the hallway. He grabbed a fistful of my nightgown from behind and shoved me down the hall in front of him. Somehow, I knew he was taking me to my mom's room at the end of the hall.

Mom's door was ajar. He pushed me through it and into the room. By the time we were halfway to Mom's bed, she was awake and had let out a scream.

"Shut up!" The man swatted her with the revolver hard enough so that I could hear the barrel connecting with the bones in her face. "If you make another sound, I'm going to rape your daughter right here in front of you. Get up, and put your shoes on."

The gunman found the light switch and turned on the overhead light. While Mom was lacing her shoes, I felt him put the barrel of the gun to the back of my head. Mom was petrified.

"As soon as your shoes are on, you will walk out your front door toward the street. I'm going to be right behind you. Do not stop to pick anything up or make any sounds. Go!"

As soon as Mom got to the front door, he stopped her.

"As you walk out the door, you'll see a car parked on the street in front of your house. Make your way toward the car. When you get there, go around to the passenger side."

We crossed the yard quickly and reached the street, where a battered green compact car was parked. He brought me around to the passenger side, where Mom was waiting.

"Get in the driver's seat. You're driving," he told Mom. Then he pushed me into the backseat and climbed in behind me.

"I'm watching you," he said menacingly to Mom as he handed her the keys to the car. "If you try to signal anyone or do anything out of the ordinary, I'll pull the trigger."

"Sir, why are you doing this?" I asked him.

"You'll find out soon enough," he growled.

We drove through the pre-dawn twilight for several miles. Our captor kept his mask on and had the gun to my ribs for the entire trip. Periodically, he would bark directions to Mom as she drove.

After we had been driving for about 25 minutes, his directions took us into a very poor neighborhood. We began to see cars in pieces or up on blocks, garbage in the streets, houses and apartment buildings with sagging structures. All the buildings had cords running every which way with clothes draped over them. I saw a miserably thin stray dog plodding through the gutter looking for scraps of food.

We made several turns as we went deeper into the neighborhood. Finally, he ordered Mom to stop the car in front of a nipa hut. It was a structure a little bigger than our living room built from bamboo poles with a thatched roof.

He pushed us in through a small doorway. The hut had a dirt floor that was strewn with beer cans and food

ALL'S WELL THAT ENDS WELL

packaging. There was a fire pit in the middle of the hut with a narrow hole in the ceiling for a chimney. A single plastic chair sat off to one side. On the opposite side was a mound of filthy bedding on the ground.

He ordered me to sit on the floor next to the chair. I did as he said, grimacing at the thought of ruining my nightgown on the dirt. He addressed Mom: "You will go to the bank and return here with 100,000 pesos," he said, using the gun as a pointer. "If any police show up here, I'll put a bullet in her head."

Mom was almost in tears. "Please, sir, don't harm my daughter! I'm going to get you your money, but I have to go home first and get my wallet to withdraw the money. Then the banks won't open for three more hours. I will have to wait."

"So you wait. Don't get stupid and call the police. You're going to give me your cell phone number, and I'm going to call you periodically. If you're on the phone with anyone, or if you don't answer promptly, I will assume you've called the police, and I'll rape your daughter. Don't place any calls to anyone. Just go to the bank, get the money and get back here. And hurry. If I think you're stalling, I'm going to rape your daughter."

"Please, sir, no. I will do everything you said."

"Go."

The next few hours stretched by intolerably as we waited. My bottom hurt from sitting on the hard ground. The man sat in the chair quietly. Gradually, daylight crept into the sky and worked its way in through the windows and door, which was open to let the cool air in. We waited in silence.

☙☙☙

Mom was frantic when she arrived home to collect her purse and cell phone. The gunman's warnings were still echoing in her head. She couldn't bring herself to call the police. Finally, she went into my room, found my phone and dialed my older sister, Esther. She answered on the first ring.

"Esther! A masked man broke into the house an hour ago. He's taken Lily and is holding her for ransom. He's ordered me to withdraw 100,000 pesos from the bank and bring it to him. I'm waiting for the bank to open. He said he would rape Lily if I contacted the police."

"Oh, my God! Why are you calling on Lily's phone?"

"Because he told me not to use my phone. He's going to call me from time to time to make sure I'm not calling anyone for help."

"Okay. Stay put. I'm going to get help. If I have to call you, I'll call Lily's phone. Keep both phones with you at all times. Don't go anywhere. I'll be there shortly."

A close friend of Esther's had nearly lost her younger sister in similar circumstances less than a year before. In that case, an organization known as *Called to Rescue* (CTR) had managed to bring the sister home unharmed. After making several phone calls, Esther managed to obtain CTR's number. She dialed it immediately.

ALL'S WELL THAT ENDS WELL

"This is Dr. Cyndi."

"Dr. Cyndi, my name is Esther. My baby sister has been kidnapped by a masked gunman and is being held for ransom. She's only 12. The kidnapper has her in a nipa hut in the Tondo district. He told my mom to go to the bank and withdraw 100,000 pesos and he'll release her."

"How does your mom know where he has her?" Dr. Cyndi asked.

"Because he brought them both there early this morning, then sent my mom out to get the money. This happened a little more than an hour ago. My mom is still waiting for the banks to open."

"Okay. I'm on it. Go right now to your mom's house and wait. I'll call you as soon as I have an update."

Dr. Cyndi called Esther back shortly after she arrived at Mom's house.

"Okay, I've been in touch with the police. They'll be ready to roll as soon as we call with information. Your mom's going to go to the bank, get the money and drive back to the hut. We'll have plainclothes officers there to grab the gunman."

"The banks aren't open yet."

"I know. We'll wait. In the meantime, stay there with your mom. Tell her not to go to the bank until we have a game plan."

CALLED TO RESCUE

Meanwhile, I sat and waited in the hut with the gunman. I was praying sporadically as I sat on the dirt floor. For some reason, I felt as though I had a fair chance of getting out of this without being killed. What I was more worried about was being raped. From the way the gunman had repeated his threat and from the tone of his voice, I got the definite impression that he wanted an excuse to do it.

The thought of being raped terrified me, not only because of the pain and the humiliation, but because it would destroy my virginity. I believed no honorable man would choose me — or even want me — after I had been raped. There was no greater desire in my heart than to be the wife of a good man someday. I would comfort him, prepare him delicious meals and tell him how handsome and strong he was. We would share a beautiful home with our children, and I would sleep in his arms every night, thanking God for him. If I were to be raped, what would become of my dream of marriage? What kind of man would have me after I had been defiled?

Being held captive was a frightening predicament, so much the worse because there was nothing I could do on my own behalf. Even Mom, who was miles away waiting for the banks to open, seemed impotent. It seemed that anything could happen. I began to pray.

Please, Lord, let me keep my purity! I promise to obey you and honor you for the rest of my life. Just please help my mom to meet this man's demands so he will let me go. Please, God, bring me out of this safely.

ALL'S WELL THAT ENDS WELL

While I prayed, the gunman sat in the chair and waited. Once, he reached into his pocket and pulled out a crinkled wrapper and unfolded it to reveal a spongy mass that looked like pagpag, discarded bits of chicken gleaned from garbage dumps, boiled and sold for pennies. I shuddered as he put handfuls of it in his mouth.

As the sun rose and warmed the air, my fears began to wane a bit as I continued to pray. On further reflection, it seemed that all this was about money, nothing more. In the two hours since I had been taken, I hadn't seen a single co-conspirator — just this lone gunman. All of his phone calls were to Mom. I was sure he was working alone. I tucked my knees to my chest and waited.

࿔࿔࿔

While I waited in the decrepit hut with the gunman, Mom, Esther, Dr. Cyndi and Dr. Cyndi's director in the Philippines, Anthony Pangilinan, worked out the logistics with the police. They had been joined by Dr. Cyndi's daughter-in-law, Mila, who is a board member of CTR and takes part in many of the rescues. One of her greater strengths is that she is Filipino. Hence, she was CTR's working authority on cultural matters, while Anthony Pangilinan was working with the Philippine national police.

Mom gave the police a recent photograph of me. Based on her recollection of the street names in the area where the kidnapper was holding me, the police set up roadblocks. The plan was for Mom to get the money out of the bank and return to the hut, where plainclothes police would ambush the kidnapper.

As soon as the banks were open, Mom drove straight to her customary branch to withdraw the money.

The teller was suspicious. "Ma'am, this is a large amount of money. May we ask why you are withdrawing so much cash?"

"I'd rather not say."

"Ma'am, you understand that we're just trying to —"

"I'd rather not say."

The teller began gathering up the bills.

One hundred thousand pesos was about $2,500 in American dollars, a great deal of money in the Philippines. Mom and Esther discussed how the gunman might have known that our family had the wherewithal to meet his demand. Mila had learned a fair amount about our family while they were preparing to rescue me, including that Esther was in medical school. That, she thought, was quite possibly the explanation. Attending medical school in the Philippines is very expensive. Unlike in America, there aren't many scholarships or student loans available, so in order to go to medical school, a person usually has to belong to a wealthier family, since it is almost always the family that pays for the tuition.

"Kidnapping for ransom is a business here," Mila informed us. "Big business. There are plenty of people who can survive on finder's fees just by hooking kidnappers up with victims. There's a good chance that

ALL'S WELL THAT ENDS WELL

this is what happened in your case — someone who attends Esther's medical school or works in administration may have taken Esther's contact information and worked outward from there. It happens all the time."

By the time Mom returned home with the money, the police were there waiting.

"Okay. Ma'am, we want you to take the money and put it in the trunk of your car. Two of our officers are going to get into the trunk of your car with the money and wait. As soon as you arrive at the hut, you will tell the gunman that you are retrieving the money from the trunk. When you open the trunk to get the money, you're going to leave the trunk lid open. My men will jump out and grab him."

There was nothing left but to go ahead with the plan. Mom and Esther prayed briefly with Mila and Dr. Cyndi. The policemen folded themselves into Mom's trunk with the money. Then Mom gathered up her purse and both cell phones and headed out.

☙☙☙

I heard Mom's car pull in at the hut. The gunman rose and grabbed the back of my nightgown.

"Get up," he said. "When we go out, you're just going to stand there and keep your mouth shut."

He peered out the window for a moment, then pushed the door open with his foot and shoved me out ahead of

CALLED TO RESCUE

him. When we were about five feet from the door, he pulled at my nightgown to stop me. I felt his gun in the small of my back.

Mom was waiting for instructions.

"Get out of the car. Bring the money," he told her.

Mom climbed out of the car and walked around the front end of the vehicle until she was standing 10 feet away from us.

"The money is in the trunk," Mom said, pointing at the car.

"Get it."

Mom walked to the rear of the car, popped the trunk and pulled a heavy white bag from it. She left the lid open and began to walk back in our direction.

I knew nothing about the police in the trunk. All I saw was Mom getting the bag out of it and walking to us.

For some reason no one could later ascertain, as soon as Mom had retrieved the money bag from the trunk, one of the plainclothes officers reached up and pulled the trunk lid shut, trapping them in there. No doubt he realized his mistake immediately, but it was already done. While it was happening, Mom heard the snick of the trunk being pulled shut. However, there was nothing she could do but go through with the exchange.

"Put the bag on the ground," the gunman ordered. Mom did as he said. As soon as he had looked inside the bag, he let go of my nightgown and told us to go.

I can't imagine how awful it was for those police officers in the trunk of Mom's car. For one thing, it had to

ALL'S WELL THAT ENDS WELL

be sweltering in there. By this time, the day had heated up to 95 degrees or more. But more than that, their suffering in the heat and confinement was a complete waste. Mom couldn't possibly open the trunk a second time without escalating the situation. The officers were accomplishing nothing except sweating all over the interior of the trunk. To make matters worse, neither of them had cell phones, so they had no way of communicating with their comrades. As I learned later, there were policemen all over the area, hiding in the bushes, waiting for a signal that never came.

Meanwhile, Mom and I got in the car and just drove off, with the policemen sweating away in the trunk. Apparently, it never occurred to Mom to pull over on the way home to let the officers out of the trunk. Or perhaps she was afraid we were being followed. Whatever the reason, the officers stayed in the trunk for the entire 25-minute drive home as the temperature exceeded 100 degrees.

We arrived home at about 11 a.m. The second we pulled into the driveway, the front door burst open, and Esther came flying out of the house. As soon as she saw me, she gave a little scream of joy and almost tackled me when I climbed out of the car. Mom ran around and joined in. We stood there hugging for a long moment.

While we were hugging and crying, the commander and his men stood off to the side, smiling but looking uncomfortable.

"I'm so glad you're back safe!" Esther said, cupping my

face with both hands. "The man didn't hurt you in any way?"

"No, he didn't touch me. He just wanted the money."

"Oh, my child!" Mom was ecstatic.

The commander shifted his weight from foot to foot and scratched his head. "Ma'am —"

"You're sure he didn't do anything to you?" Mom said.

"Mom! I promise you. Nothing happened. We just sat there and waited in the hut."

The commander gestured with his hand. "Ma'am, I hate to interrupt, but —"

"I was praying the whole time Mom was gone," Esther said. "There was no way that guy was going to hurt Lily. There were angels on this assignment!"

"Ma'am, I really need to —"

"You better believe it!" Mom declared with gusto. "Prayer changes things, let me tell you —"

"Ma'am!" the commander finally yelled. "I need to know what happened to my men!"

Mom's hands flew up to her face. "Oh, my Lord!" She ran over to the trunk and dug urgently in her purse for her keys. As she opened the trunk, I saw a look of disgust on the commander's face for just a moment. The officers climbed out lethargically, looking miserable. Their faces were drenched, and there were dark splotches on their chests and around their armpits. One of them looked particularly embarrassed, so I assume he was the one who had reached up and pulled the trunk shut during the exchange.

ALL'S WELL THAT ENDS WELL

The commander looked angry, but there was no way he was going to light into his men in front of civilians. He settled for giving them a sharp look. Then he set about putting together Plan B.

Mom was plenty unhappy about losing the money, but everyone involved considered the outcome more than satisfactory. I had been held for less than eight hours, and there wasn't a mark on me when it was over. However, we all wanted to see justice done to the kidnapper and to make all reasonable efforts to recover the money.

The gunman had managed to get well away from the area where we'd made the exchange. The hut, as it turned out, was abandoned and had been a refuge for squatters for some time. The trail had gone fairly cold, but the police persisted in their search.

In the end, it took four days to locate the gunman. The explanation was that he had several associates, though none of the others had wanted to be involved in the actual kidnapping. His partners had presumably harbored him in exchange for a share of the proceeds from the kidnapping.

When the police finally brought him into custody, they called Mom and asked us to come down to the police station to identify him.

The identification had to be accomplished through voice recognition, since the gunman had worn a mask during the whole abduction.

However, Mom and I had no trouble picking his voice out of half a dozen samples. The police had required all six men in the lineup to say a whole list of things that the gunman had actually uttered during the abduction — for example, "Open the trunk."

After the gunman was identified, we were allowed to see him. Mom and I both recognized him then. He was a handyman Mom had hired to do some remodeling work on our house. This was how he had targeted me and knew where our rooms were.

❧ ❧ ❧

From time to time, I think about how differently things might have turned out if *Called to Rescue* hadn't been there to help. The whole experience has made me grateful for what I have and for the good fortune that has followed me. I have become much more aware of the problem of sex trafficking and abduction-for-profit — both huge underworld industries that, I have been told, are too large for the modest resources of law enforcement agencies in the Philippines.

"That's why we do it," Dr. Cyndi told me not long after my own situation had been resolved. "I got tired of seeing these people get away with what they're doing. And it's not just here in the Philippines. All over the world, law enforcement agencies are under-equipped to deal with the problem. And it's no surprise; trafficking is a $32 billion industry. As we speak, 12.3 million people are in captivity. The vast majority of traffickers get away with their crimes. Their victims suffer and die unaided."

"How does this happen?" I asked.

ALL'S WELL THAT ENDS WELL

"Because people don't want to get involved. Please, don't think I'm anything special. I may be feisty, and I had some resources going in, but that doesn't mean as much as you might think. What makes me different? I made a decision to act."

A tiny little girl ran toward me. Little Emma. Her hair was washed and combed. Her dress was clean, but also hung huge on her tiny limbs. Her eyes. Oh, her eyes were so sad. So sad for such a tiny thing.

She romped toward me, threw herself on my lap and wrapped her arms tightly around my neck, before she nuzzled her face in my shoulder.

Emma was 8 years old. She came from a very poor family and had been "taken" from her front yard while her mother was in the kitchen fixing lunch. After three weeks, our workers found her in a neighborhood home. Emma had been raped repeatedly, beaten and victimized by a drug addict. Then rescued.

I hugged and loved her right back. We sat in that chair for more than an hour.

But it will take a lifetime for her to recover.

CALLING IN THE TROOPS
THE STORY OF JOY
LOCATION: THE PHILIPPINES
WRITTEN BY DOUGLAS ABBOTT

I choked back fear as the man called Jerome pushed me through the door into the decrepit building. My arms were already covered with oily streaks from his hands. But that was the least of my troubles. I was being held captive by three strange, violent men and could only guess what kind of unspeakable things they had planned for me. There was no possibility of escape. Jerome hadn't once relaxed his painful grip on my arm, and the other two were right behind me. They were all intoxicated — I could smell the sour odor of hard liquor wafting off them. Unfortunately, they were sober enough to prevent me from running off. Besides, where would I go? I was 13 years old, hundreds of miles away from home, with no money and a phone with a half-charged battery. Even if I could get away from these men, I stood a good chance of blundering into some worse horror somewhere else.

The man giving the orders was more lucid than the others. He watched me closely. He had ridden in the passenger seat of the car and fielded calls during the drive, so I knew there were others involved in whatever it was they were doing to me. I had stumbled into some well-organized enterprise of wickedness.

As I was led into the building, I saw another man emerging at the far end of the room. "Bring her back here," he said in clipped Filipino.

I heard the heavy door closing behind me, pinching off the sunlight. Then the *thock* of the deadbolt being thrown into place. I was swallowed up in the darkness of the building's interior. As my eyes adjusted to the light, I saw that all the windows were tacked over with cardboard from packing boxes. There was a single lamp burning on a table in the back, its unshaded bulb giving negligible illumination. To the left were a battered couch and a few

CALLING IN THE TROOPS

chairs clustered around a makeshift coffee table assembled from concrete blocks and a ragged piece of plywood. A radio sat on the floor next to the couch. A disjointed Latin rhythm emanated from it. The walls were bare, the particle-board floor gouged and rutted.

I could hear our footsteps echoing faintly as the music receded behind us.

As we turned into the corridor from which the fourth man had emerged, Jerome stopped and gestured ahead. "Keep going," he ordered. His voice was like dirty gravel.

On each side of the narrow hall were what appeared to be small rooms, with sheets tacked up to serve as doors. Some of the sheets billowed gently, stirred by fans which I could hear whirring. The air was thick with the odor of stale sweat. Just underneath the sound of the fans I could hear the murmur of men's voices coming from behind the sheets. *Oh, my God,* I thought. I began to feel fear like a blade in my stomach.

Up ahead, a man waited for us at the entrance to one of the rooms, his arm holding up the sheet to usher me in. As I approached, his eyes crawled over the front of my dress. I began to cry then, but I struggled not to make a sound as I was prodded into the room, where I could see a low cot with a sodden mound of bedding on it.

What in the world could I have done to deserve this? What would become of me? I began to pray harder than I ever had before: *Please, God, get me out of here!*

ಊಊಊ

CALLED TO RESCUE

The week had begun well on a bright, sunny Manila morning. I rose as usual at 7 a.m. and had a breakfast of fish and rice with Mama, Auntie, my brother Joshua and my sisters Jasmine, Mariel and Angelica. After breakfast, Mama gave each of us kids a peck on the cheek and handed us our lunches as we went out the door to catch the bus to school.

High school was fun. I enjoyed most of my classes and had little trouble with the homework. My favorite part of school was the social aspect. I had friends in each of my classes, and during the lunch period, I always ate outside at the tables with several of my best friends. There we would eat our rice and fruit under the sun, sipping Cokes and talking about everything and nothing.

A week before, there had been a new addition to our lunch group: Jessa Mae was nice and polite and gave me one of her mangoes to let me know she wanted to be friends. She lived near my house, so we would sometimes chat as we walked the same route to and from school. She always complimented me and told me she admired my intelligence. Jessa seemed fairly smart herself, though she seldom spoke in class. We had two classes together: English and Math. I felt sorry for her since she was usually alone at school and didn't seem very happy. We all wore uniforms, but hers was faded and threadbare in places, as if it had been handed down many times. I decided she needed a friend, so I made a point of including her in my activities at school.

One day, as I left for school, I saw Jessa sitting outside

CALLING IN THE TROOPS

my house. She was fiddling with loose threads on her uniform, occasionally looking up at my front door. She smiled, stood and waved as I made my way toward her.

"Morning, Jessa," I said, as I approached her.

"Morning, Joy," she replied.

I knew something was out of the ordinary by the way she was looking at me. She seemed on the verge of saying something but was having trouble getting it out.

"You want to tell me something?" I finally prodded.

Jessa nodded. "My dad gave me two tickets to see Justin Bieber in concert," she told me.

"Really?" I said. I couldn't think of any other response. There was something odd about the way she had said it. In place of exuberance, there was a weird energy about her. I didn't know a single girl who wouldn't have been jumping up and down to have two Justin Bieber tickets.

"I want you to come with me," she said.

"*What?*"

She nodded. "I want you to come with me. The concert starts at 4:00 today. It's being held at a concert hall that's only three blocks from the school. We could walk over right after our last class."

I wilted. "Jessa, I can't. My mom would light into me if I were late getting home."

"No, she wouldn't. For going to a concert? Listen, you can tell her that two of my uncles are coming with us. They'll drive you home afterward."

I hesitated, knowing full well that, even if I texted her to ask, Mama would never agree to it. The only way I could go would be to do it without asking and then hope for the best. I loved Mama and didn't often disobey her, but I was sorely tempted. I had dreamed of seeing Justin Bieber in concert ever since I was a little girl listening to my sisters' records.

"I don't know, Jessa."

"Oh, *please* come with me! I don't have anyone else to ask."

That did it. I couldn't say no. Justin Bieber, *in concert*! I couldn't believe my luck. All day long, I could scarcely focus on my schoolwork.

I pulled Jasmine aside toward the end of the day.

"Jassie, I'm not going home with you guys today. I've been invited to a concert with Jessa."

"A concert? Does Mama know about this?"

"Yes, I texted her earlier," I lied. "She said I have to be home by 6:30. I just wanted to let you and the others know. Don't worry, I'll bring you back my ticket stub."

Jasmine looked a little puzzled, but then she shook it off and smiled at me. "You lucky dog! I'm jealous."

❧❧❧

Jessa and I met outside the school at 3:30. She stood against the cinderblock wall that separated the entrance of the school from the recess yard. She was clutching her book bag and had that disturbed energy about her again. I should have been concerned, but I was too excited about the concert.

CALLING IN THE TROOPS

"There they are." Jessa pointed at a beige van in the far corner of the parking lot. It didn't occur to me to ask why Jessa's uncles didn't pull up to the door to pick us up. We threaded through the cars, cutting a jagged line toward the van. The day had grown hot and muggy. I fished a washcloth out of my bag to mop my forehead.

There were three men in the van. When they saw us coming, they smiled and waved. We made our way to the far side of the vehicle. Jessa opened the door and gestured for me to get in.

"Uncles, this is my friend Joy," she said as I was climbing into the van. "She's coming with us to the concert."

The men in the front seat turned to face me, and all three of them smiled in greeting. As Jessa got in and closed the door, I began to feel afraid. Something was wrong. That ominous energy Jessa had was all through the van. Plus, I could smell booze.

"Maybe I should call this off, Jessa. I don't want to make my mom mad." I turned to look at Jessa, but she was facing forward, impassive. I felt fear shoot through me like electricity. I turned to tell the men I was getting out, but the van was already moving.

"Please, stop the van!" I said, my voice suddenly two octaves higher. Just then, the man on my right clapped his hand over my mouth. I felt his other hand push me back into the seat. Then the man in the passenger seat was reaching back to hold my legs. I screamed and began bucking and writhing, but they were strong. My screams were muted. I tried to bite at the hand on my mouth, but he had it cupped. I looked from side to side, trying to spot someone in the parking lot, but there was no one.

"Stop struggling, little girl, or I'm going to cut you." The man spoke right into my ear. His voice was like stone. I felt his hand leave my chest, and a moment later I heard the clicking of metal as he opened his knife. He showed me the blade and then put it to my neck. I felt the sting as it broke the skin.

I was still then, praying silently as the tears came: *God, please help me. They've taken me. Please, God, help!*

༄༄༄

We drove in silence through the city. Jerome kept the knife pressed to my neck for the first 30 minutes of the drive. At one point, he switched positions and put his arm around me — to make it look more natural, I suppose.

"Just remember, girlie, if you open your mouth or make a move, I'll slice you up like a pig. We do this all the time, and we don't screw up."

I had given up on getting out of this quickly. I knew I would have to play along and wait for my opportunity. I had no idea why I had been abducted, having no frame of reference to draw from — only a vague awareness that children were sometimes kidnapped in the city. Nothing of the kind had ever happened to anyone I knew. I was a pastor's daughter living a normal middle-class life in a good neighborhood.

CALLING IN THE TROOPS

From time to time during the long, agonizing drive, I felt fresh fear pressing on me. Whenever it rose up in my throat and tears threatened, I prayed simple prayers, usually just a few words: *God, help me to get out of this.* Each time I prayed, I felt calmed, as if God was giving me his personal assurance that I was going to make it back home again.

But getting back home was a tall order. I had driven around Manila enough to know that we were getting farther and farther away from my neighborhood. Everything was unfamiliar. Gone were the handsome buildings, cut lawns and gardens full of delicate flowers. These had been replaced by broken-down shanties in dirt fields and streets filled with trash. Many of the buildings were in disrepair.

Before we left Manila, the driver stopped in front of an abandoned building to let Jessa out. I saw another vehicle parked and running nearby. I wondered who was picking her up. A real uncle, perhaps? The man in the passenger seat handed her a wad of currency. Before she got out, he gave her a warning. "Don't even think about telling anyone about this. We know where you live, and your whole family will get hurt. Just take your pay, and keep your mouth shut."

Jessa wouldn't even look at me. I thought I saw a flush of guilt on her face, mixed with fear.

As we were pulling out, I watched Jessa climb into the other car. No doubt she was headed home, where she would enjoy a hot supper and a good night's sleep. I hated her for what she had done to me. I had shown her nothing but kindness, and she had betrayed me into the hands of these violent men. God knew what they planned to do to me.

I began to cry. Soon, my cheeks were wet with tears. Why, oh, why had I disobeyed Mama? She had been wise to insist that we go straight home after school. My whole family would be frantic with worry because of me. *I'm sorry, Mama. I wish I could take it back,* I thought, as though Mama could read my mind from the other side of the city. *I won't disobey you ever again, I promise!* I wept silently as we drove on.

❧❧❧

The drive continued, long after we had passed into the country beyond Manila. My heart sank as the city receded into the distance and rice paddies were all I could see. I knew that the greater my geographical separation from home, the less likely it became that the authorities would find me. Nevertheless, I had thought to sneak a peek at Jerome's watch when his head was turned just after the beginning of the trip. We had been driving now for more than three hours and had already stopped once to fill the gas tank. I was sure that meant we still had a long ways to go. I had been watching for turnoffs and directional signs and was pretty sure that we had maintained a fairly steady direction the whole way. The men had long since settled into the drive and were scarcely paying any attention to

CALLING IN THE TROOPS

me. They seemed relaxed and even passed a flask around from time to time.

It was nine full hours before we finally left the highway and began making turns, which produced mixed emotions for me. On one hand, it meant we weren't going to get much farther away from Manila. However, I also began to feel a great sense of dread. What was going to happen to me here? They hadn't brought me all the way out here to turn around and take me home, safe and sound.

We turned into a large fenced-in property with several warehouses and a tall wrought-iron gate at the front. I saw the gate ahead and looked around furtively for landmarks. Nothing out of the ordinary on the right, but on the left, a few hundred yards in the distance, I saw three small aircraft, all facing in the same direction just off a wide graded field that was almost certainly an airstrip.

The man in the front passenger seat jumped out and pulled a key ring out of his jacket pocket, inserted a large silver-colored key into the gate lock and turned it twice, clockwise. He pushed both sides of the gate forcefully. They swayed a bit as they swung inward. Then he stepped out of the way so the van could pull into the drive.

We pulled up to a small building off to the side of the grounds. Jerome pushed me out of the car and toward the door. "Don't move," he told me, as he let go of my arm and walked around to the other side and fished keys out of his pocket. He turned the bolt and pushed the door in. As it swung open, Jerome put his hand on my back and shoved me in.

CALLED TO RESCUE

I heard Jerome lock the bolt again as I walked into the building. There were fluorescent lights hanging from the ceiling but no windows. The room was unbearably hot. Already there were great drops of sweat on my forehead. On the far side of the building was a large door on a set of tracks.

As my eyes swept to the right side of the building, my heart stopped. There, sitting against the wall, were a dozen girls, all of them young and pretty. They stared back at me with dazed, empty eyes.

Then I knew. This was a harem. I had become a sex slave.

༺༺༺

It took me half an hour to shake off my fright. I knew enough to avoid thinking about what was in store for me. That reality would engulf me soon enough. In the meantime, I was confined in this garage with a group of teenage girls who looked shell-shocked. Is that what I was going to look like? Was I actually going to be stuck here indefinitely? The answer to both of those questions seemed obvious. What basis did I have to assume I would be spared what they had experienced?

Stop it! I told myself again. The fear was warranted, but I knew instinctively that allowing my emotions to overtake me was dangerous. I had to keep praying and look for any opportunity to gain an advantage.

Then, the moment my head cleared, I remembered

CALLING IN THE TROOPS

that my captors, having been intoxicated during the kidnapping, had neglected to take my cell phone away from me. *What was I thinking?* I sat against the wall and punched a text to Mama, praying that there would be cell service in the area.

> Mama, I've been taken by three strange men. They drove me out of the city, a long ways away. I'm scared! I'm so sorry I disobeyed you, Mama. I didn't mean for this to happen. Please forgive me!

☙☙☙

I had been in that horrible warehouse for around an hour when I heard the sharp sound of the bolt being thrown on the door. Before I could even react, the girls began rising to their feet, as though on cue. I hesitated, but a girl tapped me on the shoulder. I looked up at her.

"Get up! They will be angry if you don't."

I rose quickly and stood against the wall, just as the other girls were doing. The door was thrown open, and four men walked in — the three who had taken me, plus another. I could tell immediately that the fourth man wasn't part of the ring. He was appraising us, his eyes dark with lust.

One of the other men gestured, and the stranger came closer. After a few moments, I turned my eyes to the floor. I understood clearly that this was a paying customer who was making his selection. My skin crawled. I could never have imagined this kind of depravity in a hundred lifetimes. I had seen a fiendish anticipation in his face that was terrifying. This was raw wickedness. I shuddered and began praying silently.

I heard the voice of the driver rise in volume. I looked up. He was walking toward me, looking right at me. Then he was directly in front of me. He put his hand on my shoulder and consulted the visitor.

"This one?" he asked. The visitor nodded.

I began sobbing then. "Please don't make me do this. I'm a good girl."

"Shut up!" the driver barked. "You will go with this man."

"Please!" I begged. "My family has money. They'll pay you —"

The driver's hand shot out quickly. I heard a *crack* and felt a stinging in my cheek as his palm connected hard enough to turn my head clear to the side. He turned to Jerome. "Take her to the house," he ordered.

The driver stayed behind while Jerome led me along, his hand clamped around my arm. The other two followed behind as we walked toward the main building — a large plantation-style house with straw-colored stubble all around where a lawn had been.

Jerome unlocked the front door and led me through the house toward the back corridor. As the double row of rooms came into view, I tried to steel myself, even as I prayed. Part of me still couldn't believe that this kind of thing went on, *anywhere*. What kind of men were these? How could God allow people like this to draw breath?

CALLING IN THE TROOPS

Why are you letting this happen to me, God? I prayed. *Can't you see what's going on here?*

The man at the end of the hall lifted one of the curtains and gestured for me to go into the room. I wanted to plead with him, but I still felt the stinging in my cheek. As I walked under the sheet, he addressed Jerome: "Escort our guest back in five minutes." Jerome nodded and left.

The room was about 10 feet by six. There was nothing in it except a twin bed, a small table with a lamp and a fan stirring the muggy air from the corner. My captor entered the room behind me and let the sheet down. There would only be one sheet on the bed …

"My name is Angelo," he said in a low voice that was gentler than the others' had been. "I know you're scared. This situation isn't as bad as you think. We're not monsters, and we're not going to keep you here forever. If you do well for us, we'll send you home soon. I promise." He smiled then, displaying a mouthful of blackened stumps. "I have something that will help you relax."

He gestured at the bed. "Sit down." I did as I was told.

Angelo pulled a black vinyl case out of his pocket and set it on the table. He drew the zipper and opened it to reveal a hypodermic needle and a soot-covered teaspoon. Even though I had never seen one of these kits before, I felt a dark vibe just looking at it.

"What's that?" I asked him.

"It's medicine. You'll feel a lot better. Trust me."

I knew "medicine" was a euphemism for drugs, which I wanted no part of. My parents had warned me about the horrors of drug abuse and had even shown me pictures of addicts in the throes of their disease. I had long ago resolved never to touch drugs. However, I knew just as well that I wouldn't be given a choice in the matter. I wasn't particularly convinced by Angelo's nice-guy performance. It wouldn't take much to get slapped again or worse. I was stuck.

I tried not to watch as he went through the ritual of preparing the dose, but I was fascinated in spite of myself. He poured a bit of powder into the bowl of the spoon, added water and put a flame underneath it. Soon the darkening water was bubbling and making little popping noises. Then he popped a wad of cotton into the reddish-brown liquid, put the tip of the needle into the cotton and drew the substance up. He held the needle up and flicked the side, then pushed the plunger up, sending a bit of liquid shooting out of the tip.

"I don't want to do this," I said meekly, hoping against reason that he would let me out of it.

"It will help you," he said implacably. I heard just a hint of warning in his voice.

I prayed and shut my eyes as he tapped the inside of my arm, found a vein and plunged the needle in. A moment later, I felt a tingling warmth in my head and chest that spread quickly into my stomach and then my loins. I heard a faint buzzing in my ears. It felt as though my brain were being tickled by a feather. I felt a peace like I had known when my father rocked me to sleep as a young child. My whole body felt good.

CALLING IN THE TROOPS

I heard Angelo chuckle. I opened my eyes and saw him looking at me, smiling.

"What did I tell you?" he said. "Relaxing, isn't it?"

I said nothing. I found it startlingly enjoyable. There wasn't the slightest pain anywhere in my body. I was warm from head to toe. The distress I had felt over my current predicament was still there, but I was detached from it. Even the fear of what was about to happen to me had receded into the background, like a newspaper headline I had gotten rid of by simply folding the paper and stowing it away.

Angelo chuckled again and began packing up the needle and spoon. "A man is going to come in and spend some time with you," he told me. "He's not going to hurt you. Be nice to him. If you treat our friends nicely, we'll let you go home very soon." He smiled again, showing his broken teeth, then rose and walked out.

The man who had selected me in the garage came in a moment later. As he approached the bed, I remember praying, *God, help me to be nice to this man so I can go home.*

While he was grunting on top of me, I kept praying. *Father, bring me home soon.* The horror of what was happening to me was muted because of the drugs. Little did I know how awfully clear it would be to me later on. I thought of Mama and Papa, Auntie, my sisters and my brother. *Lord, take care of them. Don't let them worry too much about me.*

It was over before I knew it.

CALLED TO RESCUE

☙☙☙

"There are twice as many girls as there were when I got here," Nina said. She was a petite girl with blond highlights in her hair who had struck up a conversation with me the morning of my second day. "Don't keep to yourself," she had said. "It's much harder that way." And she was right. I felt better after I had talked with her for a while. Now, however, the drugs had worn off, and she was telling me distressing things.

"They told me they were going to send me home months ago. They tell all the girls that," Nina said. "Do you see that girl with the birthmark on her cheek? That's Nicole. She's been here for eight months. She kept track by making scratches on the wall with a nail."

I asked Nina how often they had injected her.

"Every time I go over there," she said. "Same as all the girls."

I said nothing for a long while. I remembered how much I had loved the feeling of euphoria I had gotten from the drug, which Nina informed me was heroin. I had enjoyed the experience even knowing how dangerous it was. I wondered how many girls learned to like being picked out by the visiting men because of how our captors had paired sex with heroin. I noticed how some of the girls smiled flirtatiously when visitors were brought to the garage.

We sat in the corner, watching the other girls play cards and board games. Nina told me about her whole

CALLING IN THE TROOPS

family. She had three brothers and two sisters. Her father was a policeman in Manila. "He got promoted to sergeant just before I came here," she said.

Nina and I spent the whole day talking about our families and our lives "before." She was a sweet girl, but I sensed somehow she had grown bitter during her time here. I wondered if the same thing would happen to me. *No,* I promised myself. *The Lord will get me out of here, I know he will.* I couldn't allow myself to think about all these other girls, some of whom had been here for months, like Nina and Nicole. Surely God loved them, too, didn't he? But these were matters too weighty to think about. It was crucial to remain positive and focus on doing whatever I could to hasten my escape.

Whenever the men came and we all stood up for appraisal, I felt a fresh stab of fear, thinking I might have to go with another man. I was terrified to discover that the idea wasn't entirely unpleasant to me if it meant another taste of that heavenly drug. However, I wasn't selected. Nina and I were left alone that whole day. I refused to watch as different girls were led away to the house and that awful hallway full of rooms. I prayed for them instead.

It was midnight when they threw a switch, and the lights in the ceiling went out. Nina and I were already stretched out, facing each other. We were starting to fall asleep but still talking in snatches.

"Goodnight, Nina." I reached out and squeezed her hand.

Nina squeezed back.

CALLED TO RESCUE

The morning came suddenly. I awoke with a start and looked up. Nina was nudging me with her toe. "Get up!" she whispered. All the other girls were standing. I stood quickly and looked over toward the door. Jerome was back, hauling another girl in. She looked like she was around 15, very pretty, her eyes red from crying. She looked terrified.

Thus began another day.

❧❧❧

Little did I know, my entire family was praying fervently for my rescue back at home. Mama had supplied police with all the details she could, but it was very little and there hadn't been an inch of progress. They had contacted everyone they or the police could think of. They had applied for and been denied assistance from various agencies, including the military. My family was discovering firsthand how inadequate the resources were against the powerful sex trafficking industry in the Philippines.

After two frantic days, my uncle, who everyone refers to as Pastor Johnny, remembered that one of his former professors, Dr. Cyndi Romine, with whom he had remained in touch, was founder and leader of *Called to Rescue*, an international organization that dealt with abductions like mine.

Because of my abduction into the sex trafficking industry and CTR's subsequent involvement, my family

CALLING IN THE TROOPS

set about learning everything they could about the organization. Dr. Romine established *Called to Rescue* as an entity in the Philippines in 2008. The group's director, Anthony Pangilinan, is the brother of a senator and is connected with many other influential people. Two years after its Philippines operation was established, CTR was given an official invitation to visit the Senate floor. Fifteen people from the organization spent the day sitting in on Senate hearings and meeting personally with several senators who were concerned about the scourge of sex trafficking in the Philippines, where 250,000 children live on the streets and 100,000 are trafficked into sex slavery each year.

Thanks to its work with so many influential people, CTR has established a considerable foothold in the Philippines, a country of 95 million people with many economic, socio-cultural and spiritual challenges. God has been with CTR from the beginning, opening doors that otherwise could never have budged.

One huge milestone came in a single day, when Dr. Cyndi received an invitation to visit the vice president's office. During that visit, Vice President Binay seated Dr. Romine and her delegation at a conference table with members of the presidential cabinet. Represented there were the Department of Health, Department of Justice, Department of Education and the Department of Social Welfare and Development. Also present were key members of the Philippine government's own task force: Inter-Agency Council Against Trafficking (IACAT), which was seeking to improve the Tier Rating for the Philippines (and has done so since), as well as its overall effectiveness.

Through events such as this, CTR has gained proximity and influence with the Philippine authorities, enabling it to wield a formidable counterweight against the national epidemic of sex trafficking.

Dr. Cyndi was in the United States when she received an e-mail from Pastor Johnny, who leads a church in Manila:

> Dr. Romine, my niece, Joy, has been kidnapped. We believe her abductors are sex traffickers. The police here have been unable to locate her. Please help!

Dr. Cyndi and her staff mobilized quickly for what was to become one of the most exhaustive, protracted rescues her organization has ever undertaken. None of the people involved — and there were many — stopped to consider what would be required of them. The rescue would end up lasting seven days. All measures had to be coordinated between the United States and the Philippines. Activity on both ends went on around the clock.

Dr. Cyndi coordinated with Philippine authorities. Her daughter-in-law, Mila, also a CTR board member, exchanged information with my family. Within a few hours, Anthony Pangilinan had contacted the head of IACAT, as well as the Philippine National Police (PNP) and the National Bureau of Investigation (NBI — the

CALLING IN THE TROOPS

Philippines' version of the FBI). Within a day, the rescue effort involved no fewer than 100 men from these agencies, as well as members of the local police force. According to the *Manila Times*, after all was said and done, it was the largest manhunt in the history of the Philippines.

࿆࿆࿆

Mila's first steps were to request recent photographs of me and to instruct my family to text me to ask for any details of my surroundings I might have observed. Mama was so distraught she could not communicate well, so Auntie took over texting and coordinating with Mila.

Initially during the ordeal, the only texts I had received from my family were short inquiries asking if I was okay. Now, following the engagement of CTR, I received a very encouraging text from Auntie:

> Joy, there are many people looking for you. We are praying and are confident we will bring you back home soon. Don't lose hope! Tell me anything you can about the area you were brought to. Did you notice any landmarks? After you have texted me back, shut your phone off and save your batteries. We are coming to get you!

I texted back:

> I don't know where I am, but I think we've traveled about nine hours. They brought me to a fenced-in compound with a big iron gate and

CALLED TO RESCUE

several buildings on the property. The compound is guarded by men with rifles. They drove me in a beige van. When we were pulling in, I saw what looked like an airport nearby. There were three small planes, the prop kind. Auntie, please hurry!

Anthony Pangilinan took that information and relayed it to his government contacts, who dispatched their men in turn to research the locations of all the airports within the radius. It was quickly determined that I must have been taken north of Manila. A cursory examination of area maps revealed a small airport about nine hours north. Immediately, the bulk of the team mobilized for the rescue headed north. Auntie went with them.

Meanwhile, investigators took my photos to the high school and the surrounding area to determine if anyone had seen anything the day I was abducted. They could find no one.

The photographs were then used to print flyers, which were posted everywhere throughout my neighborhood and the area around the school. There was an added sense of urgency because of the fact that two days had gone by before anything of substance had been accomplished. Now they were pulling out all the stops. All the while, the texts flew back and forth as new information came in.

❦❦❦

Not quite half a day after I sent Auntie the text describing the airport and the compound, half a dozen

CALLING IN THE TROOPS

men charged into the warehouse where we were, flipping lights on and yelling at the top of their lungs. The overhead door at the far side of the garage began opening slowly, rumbling and creaking as it went up. The next thing we knew, a large box truck had pulled up to the doors. More men hopped out, some with rifles and all of them moving urgently. They began herding us all into the back of the truck.

Within a few minutes, the warehouse was empty, and the truck was moving. I could see nothing from the back of the truck, since the rear door had been closed and latched. I could only hear the sounds of the tires spraying gravel, men shouting, doors slamming. Then we were moving and didn't stop for a long time.

☙☙☙

The IACAT and NBI, accompanied by Auntie and some local police, arrived at the compound to find it deserted. It was immediately obvious that some well-placed informants had tipped off the kidnappers. Back home, Mama and the others were dismayed. It was as if I had been kidnapped all over again. However, Mila assured them in a text that CTR and its friends weren't giving up. "We will find her. Keep praying! You will see Joy again!"

My family never stopped praying. They fasted, too. I can't imagine the hardship they endured during that weeklong rescue effort. Besides food, they were also deprived of sleep, except for the inconsequential moments

CALLED TO RESCUE

of rest they were able to catch between texts and calls. They truly shared my suffering.

Meanwhile, up north, we arrived at the outskirts of a different city. The rear door of the truck came open again, and the men moved us into a large house, where we were again confined under lock and key. This time I wasn't so lucky; I saw no distinctive landmarks to report to Auntie.

Without a description of the new location, the authorities went from place to place, asking people questions and showing my photograph. They waited for the tips to come in. A couple of days later, they texted Auntie:

> We have tracked your niece and her captors to a house in Tuguegarao. We are making all haste and are hopeful of surprising them there.

Everyone was optimistic. The operation had gathered momentum and intensity. Most significantly, investigators had actually found a smoldering trail at the compound and expected to close the deal at the second location. But it wasn't that easy. After we had spent only a couple of days at the house in Tuguegarao, the men again rounded us up and loaded us back into the trucks. We were off again, headed for places unknown.

There was no small commotion among the girls as to what all this activity might mean. We knew it could simply have been some kind of reorganization taking place, with the house serving as a staging area. However, I had a strong sense that my captors were dealing with some

CALLING IN THE TROOPS

serious problems. Their demeanor and movements were frantic. Moreover, they were angry. While we were being loaded up for the drive out of Tuguegarao, a captain of the operation began screaming at the men. I overheard some of it.

"… told you to charge your goddamn phone! Now get all this packed up, and quit screwing around …" The captain hauled off and slapped one of them so hard that I heard a *crack* from 100 yards away. Then, enraged, he pointed his rifle into the air and discharged several rounds. The men scattered like frightened cats.

I began to feel a stirring in my spirit. I thought this ordeal might well have a happy ending, and I prayed all the harder. I was still sending periodic texts to Auntie, but I was more mindful than ever about conserving the negligible battery juice I had left.

Meanwhile, back in Manila, Mama received a fresh text from Auntie:

> They've slipped through the net again. Will keep you apprised of developments.

I am told that when this news came, Mama made a sound that was somewhere between a moan and a wail. She had been sure this text would mean I'd been rescued.

Dr. Cyndi, Mila, Anthony Pangilinan and his team came to the sober realization that they were contending with a remarkably well-informed opposition.

"There's nothing to do but forge ahead," Mila told my family. "The authorities are canvassing the neighborhood

CALLED TO RESCUE

in Tuguegarao. We're gaining on them all the time. They can't keep this up forever."

☙☙☙

They couldn't keep it up forever, but it seemed like forever. Since the tumult had begun, I had lost track of days and nights. The men were increasingly on edge and chattering constantly on their cell phones.

By this time, I was certain that the authorities were on our trail and probably getting closer, if our frantic, disjointed movements were any indication.

Once again, we replayed a now-familiar scenario. After another long drive, we were again unloaded and herded into another nondescript house. I was frightened that at some point, things might escalate dangerously. These people clearly didn't have any regard for our lives. If things got too tight, what was to prevent them from putting bullets into our heads and cutting their losses? At the same time, I was gratified to see that considerable pressure was being placed on them. There was no longer any question but that the net was tightening.

In fewer than 48 hours, we were again loaded into trucks and whisked away. As I learned later, the authorities descended on our third location just an hour later and found nothing. It is still not known whether their tips had led them to the wrong building or whether they had simply not arrived quickly enough.

Once again, I found myself curled up in the back of an

CALLING IN THE TROOPS

industrial truck, my body aching from lying on the corrugated metal floor, sweating profusely in the intense heat. The only light we had came into the truck through several coin-sized holes that had been punched into the sides, presumably for air circulation.

This time, the trip was long and arduous. The hours crawled by. My neck, back and hips were screaming from days of confinement in makeshift spaces. By this time, my cell phone had been discovered and confiscated. Just before I lost it, I managed to send a last text to Auntie:

> We're moving again.

The men had supplied us with plastic cups and a bucket of drinking water. I began to feel nauseous and wondered whether the water was sanitary. However, I had no choice but to drink it; the stifling heat in the back of the truck kept me perpetually thirsty. Periodically, the truck would pull off the road. When it did, Jerome would hustle us out to squat in the bushes and relieve ourselves.

The trip stretched on for so long that I wondered if we were returning to Manila. From my captors' perspective, it made no sense to hurtle straight into the scene of the crime — and the functioning command center of the investigation. Nevertheless, I knew some Philippines geography and could think of nowhere else it would take so long to reach.

Over that long trip, I began to lose heart. My body hurt. I missed my family terribly. I began to doubt

CALLED TO RESCUE

whether the authorities would catch up with us. There was no more doubt in my mind that we had been moved these three times in an effort to elude a rescue operation. Nothing else made sense. But instead of being swept up in the net, my kidnappers had gotten out of it — three times now. I began to despair of ever being rescued.

God, are you going to bring me home? I asked. I didn't get an answer.

༺༻

I was jolted out of sleep, still sprawled in the back of the truck. We had stopped. I rubbed my eyes and looked around. The other girls were gone. I was all by myself. I heard doors opening and closing and the crunching of boots on gravel. Then the rear door of the truck was raised. It was Jerome. He gestured at me to get out.

As soon as my feet hit the ground, his hand was on my arm again. To my right was a huge house, a mansion by Philippines standards, to my left the grounds — several acres lush with papaya, banana and coconut trees. We walked along an intersecting drive that led toward a small outbuilding perhaps 100 feet from the house. As we climbed the stairs, a plump woman wearing an apron opened the door for us. She looked me over and nodded at Jerome.

Just before he turned and walked back toward the truck, Jerome tightened his grip on my arm and issued me a warning: "If I were you, I wouldn't cause any trouble.

CALLING IN THE TROOPS

We're 20 minutes away. You would be well advised to keep your mouth shut, and do what you're told." Then he was gone.

The woman brought me back to the rear of the house, where the kitchen was. My stomach rumbled in response to the smells of cooking food. I hadn't had a bite to eat for hours. She told me to sit at the small table.

"My name is Pia," she said, settling into a chair across from me.

"Mine's Joy," I replied politely.

"I know," she said, cryptically leaving it at that. While I digested this, she sat looking at me with a serious expression on her face that I couldn't interpret.

I was thoroughly mystified. After everything I had experienced at the hands of my captors over the last several days, now here I was, sitting in a comfortable kitchen with a woman who appeared to be harmless. Jerome had left. None of those hideous men was about. Why was I here? How did this woman fit into the scheme? I could not explain the turn of events. Nevertheless, I was still under duress. There was no possibility of my simply getting up and leaving.

She saw me eyeing the steaming pans on the stove. "Are you hungry?" she asked.

"Oh, yes, ma'am. Starving!"

She dished up a big bowl of rice and fried eggs, set it in front of me, then sat back down without dishing up food for herself. I dug into the rice hungrily. It was the best meal I'd eaten since my capture. I glanced up between bites. She was just sitting there watching me eat.

When I had finished, she brought my bowl to the sink and returned to the table. I felt at ease, both because of the rice and Pia's demeanor. She did not seem hard or threatening at all. Periodically, she would get up and stir the pots on the stove and then come back to the table.

"Do you own this place?" I asked her.

"No. I'm the cook. These are my quarters."

"Do you like your job?"

"Yes, I like it very much."

It was just small talk, but I had started to like her. I sensed that the feeling was mutual. She smiled at me from time to time as we talked between her trips to the stove.

"I'm sure you've noticed that we've had some issues at the places you've been to," Pia said finally, ending the small talk. "That's why you're here."

This was getting weirder and weirder. I couldn't imagine who this woman was.

"I imagine you must be missing your family."

"Oh, I miss them so much! I wish there were some way I could talk to my mom and Auntie. They're worried sick about me!"

She just looked at me.

I pressed on. "Do you think you could permit me to make just one short call home?"

She sighed heavily and just kept looking at me.

"Please? Oh, please! I promise I won't tell them anything that could get you into trouble. I swear!"

She sighed again. "Okay. Make it quick. There's a

CALLING IN THE TROOPS

phone on the counter over there," she said, pointing behind her.

I was elated, particularly since the irony of the situation wasn't lost on me: I had been kidnapped, brutalized, injected with drugs and raped. Now, all of a sudden, this strange woman was feeding me rice and permitting me the use of her phone. It had to be some kind of bizarre mistake. There was no way I was getting out of my predicament this easily. I remembered Nina and Nicole, who had both been held for multiple months. It didn't make sense that they would treat me any differently.

Haven't you been praying for a way back home? The question reverberated in my head with uncanny clarity. In fact, I *had* been praying for a way home. I was certain my family had been praying as well. Could things possibly have turned around this quickly?

There was only one way to find out.

I dialed Mama's cell number, although it was Auntie who answered it. She picked up on the second ring.

"Hello?"

"Auntie, it's me."

"Joy! Oh, my God!" She held the phone to her chest for a moment. I heard her muted voice yelling for my sisters. "Jasmine! Girls! It's Joy!" Then she was speaking into the phone again. "Baby, where are you? Are you all right?"

"I'm fine, Auntie." I lowered my voice so as not to be overheard. "I'm in a big house in a wealthy neighborhood. I feel like I'm close to home."

CALLED TO RESCUE

I gave Auntie as many more details about the place as I could think of and told her again that I was fine.

"We thought you'd lost your phone since we hadn't heard from you," Auntie said.

"I did. I'm using the phone at the house here."

"What?"

"Yeah. Weird, huh? This lady seems very nice. Anyway, Auntie, I promised I would keep this short. I'm sure she'll let me call again. I should go now. Tell everyone I'm fine."

Auntie reluctantly said goodbye, and the conversation ended.

Fifteen minutes later, Pia astonished me by asking me to dial Auntie again.

"What on earth for?" I asked.

She had a resolute look on her face. "I need to speak with her. I'm going to take you home."

It was too strange for me to believe at first. What I didn't yet know was that the effort to find me had grown into an international operation involving three federal agencies and more than 100 men. As Dr. Cyndi would put it later, "They kidnapped the wrong girl." *Called to Rescue* had mobilized a force on my behalf that was threatening to overturn the entire sex ring. At this point, they wanted to be rid of me, and Pia was taking steps to make that happen.

A moment later, she was on the phone with Auntie.

"… Yes, we have her here in Manila … Yes, she is quite all right. I fed her some lunch just a little while ago.

CALLING IN THE TROOPS

She is a charming girl ... No, the reason I'm calling is because I want to set things right. We were wrong to do what we did. We're not monsters ... Yes. Please put Joy's mother on the phone."

While I listened in amazement, Pia made arrangements to meet Mama at a shopping mall, where she would release me to her.

I still wasn't sure this was for real, but two hours later, Pia and I were pulling out of the driveway in her car. I can't describe the flood of relief and joy I felt on the way to the mall.

It was just after 4 p.m. when we pulled into the parking lot of Shoemart. Pia and I walked together to the entrance and went in. I had heard her specify that we would meet Mama in a small coffee shop near the entrance. As we approached the area, I spotted Mama and Auntie standing at one of the tables. Mama had already seen us. She had her hands over her mouth. I could hear her wailing with relief. Then she was running to meet me. Auntie was right behind her.

I bumped several people as I ran to meet Mama. I had never been so happy to see anyone in my whole life. All three of our faces were wet with tears as I ran into Mama's arms. Auntie joined the hug from the side.

"Oh, my baby! My baby!" Mama was sobbing.

Our reunion was interrupted by the sound of men's voices yelling and people making surprised noises all around us. I turned to see what was happening.

Pia was surrounded by plainclothes police officers and

CALLED TO RESCUE

IACAT agents. They were pointing their service revolvers at her and ordering her to get on the floor. As we watched, she lowered herself to the floor, facedown, right in her $300 designer jeans. The police put her wrists in handcuffs and hauled her back to her feet. Her face was grey and chalky. There was terror in her eyes as they escorted her out of the building.

After she had been taken away, several IACAT officials approached us. They all had huge smiles on their faces.

"You don't know how happy we are to see you, Joy!" the commander said. Mama couldn't speak; she was still weeping. Auntie hugged the commander. All of them stepped up to shake my hand. I was a little embarrassed at the outpouring. Now that the ordeal was over, I felt a rush of happiness. Mama clutched my hand almost hard enough to make me wince. I couldn't stop thanking the officers.

"You're welcome!" the commander said heartily. "And, Miss Joy, we especially want you to meet this gentleman." He did a half turn and extended his hand behind and to his right, where a tall, thin man was standing quietly. "Joy, this is Anthony Pangilinan. He was working closely with *Called to Rescue*."

"What's that?" I asked as Mr. Pangilinan stepped forward to shake my hand.

He smiled, and I could feel the warmth in his grasp. "I'm going to tell you all about them," he said. "They are the reason you're standing here right now."

Mr. Pangilinan and his wife invited the three of us —

CALLING IN THE TROOPS

Mama, Auntie and me — to dinner. "I have a great deal to tell you," he said. "This is going to take some time." He waved away Mama's offer to pay for the dinner. "No, ma'am. This is my treat. I've been waiting for this moment for a week. And what a week it's been!" He was handsome and charming, and there was nothing we could do except allow him to whisk us away to a quiet air-conditioned diner, where he told me all about CTR, its mission and scope. Even Mama and Auntie learned new things in spite of having already been told a great deal about the organization.

"This lady is going to want to hear from you," Mr. Pangilinan said, setting a business card and a brochure on the table and sliding them over to me.

The moment I got home, I used Mama's phone to call Dr. Cyndi. My own phone was still in Jerome's pocket. I was quite surprised to learn that the number on the business card was her personal cell number.

"This is Dr. Cyndi," she answered.

"Hi, Dr. Cyndi. This is Joy."

Dr. Cyndi responded with loud, exultant noises.

"You saved my life," I told her, trying to keep from crying again. "I'll never be able to thank you enough!"

"You already have," she said. "You're back home safe with your family. That's why I do this. And if you want to do more, send me a text from time to time telling me what's happening with you. I feel like you're my daughter now." I heard the tears in her voice.

There were many conversations that followed. I called

CALLED TO RESCUE

Mila the following day. She described the rescue from her perspective and explained that Pia was the leader of the entire sex trafficking ring.

"But why would she walk right into a police ambush?" I asked.

"In our culture, as you have learned somewhat, there is a strong emphasis on reciprocating gestures of goodwill. She really thought that since she was voluntarily bringing you back, your mother would let her off the hook out of gratitude. She was mistaken."

I was ecstatic to be home, but there was hardship ahead. I was brought into protective custody while criminal proceedings were brought against everyone involved in the trafficking ring. During that time, I lived at a safe house for many months, which is another story in itself. We never found out what happened to Nina, Nicole and the other girls.

I live with the feeling that I owe Dr. Cyndi and Mila and all the others a debt of gratitude I can never repay. I have told Dr. Cyndi this, and she jokes, "Fantastic. That means you can't ever stop writing and texting me to let me know how you are."

And so I haven't. I just sent her a text recently.

> Hello, Ma'am Cyndi,
>
> I'm Joy ... the one you visited last November 2011 in the safe house in the Philippines and one of the girls you've helped to be rescued from trafficking. I've been looking for your profile since last year after my discharge from the safe house.

CALLING IN THE TROOPS

I just want to thank you again, for God has used you to regain what I have lost.

I'm now in college after passing my acceleration exam.

You're a big part of my life-changing experience, and I will forever cherish your kind heart for girls like me. You are such a blessing, and may God bless you and your family.

I'll be very happy to see you again ... Thank you!

Joy

While walking the cement caverns called streets and alleys of cities around the world, the Lord and I find one ... one person to rescue.

— *Dr. Cyndi Romine*

THE GIRL ON THE BANK
THE STORY OF DR. CYNDI ROMINE
WRITTEN BY MARTY MINCHIN

As our outrigger canoe glided up to the Pagsanjan Falls, I whipped my head to the right to glance at an out-of-place trio on the shore.

Is that a drug deal going down?

A tall Caucasian man, casually dressed in shorts and a polo shirt, spoke intently with a Filipino couple. The man and woman looked like many of the local people we'd encountered in our first month of living in a suburb of Manila, the capital of the Philippines. They clearly weren't wealthy. The man had on a t-shirt and jeans, the uniform of poor Filipino men. The woman wore a blouse and long skirt in the typically modest local style.

The fair-haired foreigner handed a stack of bills to the couple. Not wanting to stare rudely, I turned my gaze back to the water. The rainforest canopy on the sides of the river was growing greener and more lush, indicating that we were getting closer to the falls.

CALLED TO RESCUE

I couldn't help but look back at the scene playing out on the river's edge. To my surprise, like a magician yanking a rabbit from a hat, the woman pulled a young child from behind her skirt and handed her to the foreigner. The girl was 3 or 4 years old.

No.

The couple turned their backs and walked away, and the tall blond man picked up the child and tossed her in the air. The little girl looked like she was laughing at the game.

No.

The scene moved behind me as the outrigger glided forward, but I looked again over my shoulder and confirmed my fears. What I saw changed me forever.

"Did you see that?" I mouthed to my husband, Greg. Tears already were welling in my eyes and overflowing down my cheeks. My stomach churned with shock and disgust. I vomited over the side of the canoe into the water.

The bold foreign man may have believed the landscape screened him, but I could see enough to know what was happening. I watched helplessly as he pushed the little girl down on the rocks. He was raping her.

If the child screamed, I couldn't hear her over the sounds of the water.

༄༄༄

THE GIRL ON THE BANK

We can buy an infant for $30 U.S. currency, the same price of 2 ounces of cocaine on the street. If we don't, a sex trafficker will.

☙☙☙

Having lived in San Francisco, which has a large Asian population, I'd heard about the sex trafficking of children across the Pacific. From the little I knew, I believed it primarily happened over there. I knew the victims usually were young girls. However, I never expected to witness it firsthand on an excursion at a popular tourist destination during our first month overseas. I certainly never thought it could happen to a child that young.

Greg and I moved to the Philippines with his job in 1988. We settled into a well-to-do section of Manila, and we had intended to focus most of our lives there. However, the rape of the little girl drastically altered my outlook. When I saw children on the streets, I wondered about their stories. What did they eat? Where did they sleep? Where were their parents? Who were they with at night?

Not long after my experience at Pagsanjan Falls, Greg and I visited a friend in Olongapo City, a port city made popular during the Vietnam War by the many American soldiers who took R&R there. We decided to explore the city one evening during our visit. We started in the outdoor food market, where bins of brightly colored tropical fruits lined the walkway. The streets were crowded with late-night traffic, cars and brightly decorated Jeepneys (Filipino buses) that honked and wove around the bicycles that darted in and out of the lanes.

As the evening darkened into late night, the children roaming the streets remained. They did not go home to snuggle up safe in bed. Some picked their dinner out of a gutter before settling into a doorway or on a step for the night. Others eventually disappeared, and I couldn't help but wonder who might be brutalizing them that night. My eyes had been opened. I knew that there was little chance these children were sleeping soundly.

These kids didn't appear to be native Filipino. Some looked Caucasian, others African-American. We guessed that they primarily were between ages 5 and 8. Because of the American military presence in Olongapo City, many people there spoke English. We nosed around, asking questions about these roaming children. Some were the offspring of prostitutes who had abandoned them. Many had American military fathers who either didn't know about them or didn't care.

These children, I would learn, were just one facet of the world of poverty and depravity lying just beneath the surface of polite society in the Philippines. You can't truly grasp the depths and enormity of this kind of evil all at once, though. If I had seen the whole picture instantly, I probably would have died of sorrow.

☙ ☙ ☙

THE GIRL ON THE BANK

When evil comes in like a flood, there should always be a force that rises above that evil and conquers it.

❧❧❧

"Hey, you kids! Get off my steps!" Pastor Roberto yelled at the boys who were asleep and blocking his door in Olongapo City. "Get out of here. You're such a nuisance!"

They looked back from the steps, big brown eyes staring from white faces. Their scalps crawled with lice, and they were filthy and neglected.

"Older Brother, where are we supposed to go?"

"Where are we supposed to sleep?"

Pastor Roberto walked inside with a heavy heart, their questions echoing in his head. *Where were they to go?*

His concern for these children grew, and he began taking them in for shelter.

Irrevocably changed by the girl on the banks of the river, who I'd been unable to help, I was determined to navigate this maze of street children and provide food, shelter, education and love for as many as I could. They needed a home and a safe place to grow up.

We soon connected with Pastor Roberto over our shared determination to change the fate of these children. We helped him move into a larger house, bought him a car and established a safe house for street children.

The children often came to the house without ages, names or birthdays. Many chose their own names. To determine how old they were, I would have them open their mouths so I could count their molars. When I asked them what birthday they'd like to have, many wanted to know when Jesus was born. There were quite a few December 25 birthdays.

They told us about their lives. As their stories unfolded, I saw the devastating effects of poverty. Parents selling their children or videotaping them in sexual situations so they could buy a little food. Mothers prostituting themselves to earn a living or leaving their children on the street because they couldn't afford to feed them.

After a while, word got out that we were operating a safe house for children. One day a Filipino woman, a prostitute, showed up at our door with her two children.

"I'm going to the market," she explained. "Can you watch them?"

I looked down at the 4 year old and the infant in a baby carrier.

"What time do you think you'll be back?" She was silent and avoided my gaze. I tried again.

"What are their names?"

"The boy is Stephan, and the girl is Lisa."

"Which market are you going to?"

Again, no answer. The woman pushed Lisa's carrier at me and retreated down the steps. I took Stephan's hand and led him into the safe house. Just as I suspected, the mom never returned.

Eight years later, I asked Stephan what the safe house

THE GIRL ON THE BANK

meant to him. He looked at me quizzically. "I mean, what does living here all your life mean to you?"

He started sobbing. "It's my home." Of course it was.

One of my quests was to find the U.S. military men who fathered these orphans and ask them to provide money to support the kids. We were happy to keep the children in the safe house if the dads didn't want them, but the money would be helpful in running our organization.

I became an expert at finding these fathers, sometimes with nothing but a first name the child pulled from memory.

One boy knew his dad's last name was Williams. The boy had lived with his mom and dad in Olongapo City until he was 6 years old, and when the parents decided to return to the United States, they left him and his two siblings on the street in the Philippines.

I miraculously located the dad in the United States. All I needed from him was a signature.

"You are a U.S. citizen, and you have three children here in the Philippines," I explained over the long-distance call. "If you sign these forms, your kids can get a U.S. passport."

"I'm not paying one dime for those kids," he retorted.

"Look, we will take care of them. I just need you to sign these papers and mail them to us."

"I told you, I'm not spending a dime on them."

I could tell he meant that literally.

"I will send you the forms and a self-addressed

stamped envelope." I had to make it as easy as possible. "Just sign the papers and drop the envelope in the mail."

A stamp at that time cost 30 cents. This man didn't even want to spend that much on his children.

To my great surprise, the father actually did sign and return the papers, but he never made contact with the kids. They grew up in our safe house.

Of course, not all fathers responded this way.

The mother of Hans, one of our Caucasian-looking kids, knocked on the safe house door one day to tell me she knew who Hans' father was.

"What's his name?" I asked.

She knew his first and last name, which was very unusual, and the city where he lived. After a quick search, I found his phone number.

"Sir, I'm Dr. Cyndi Romine, and I think I have your son in a safe house in Olongapo City."

The silence on that line lasted several minutes, which is an excruciatingly long time when you are on the phone.

The dad began to cry.

"I know you are probably not going to believe this, but I was the best guy on the ship. I was only with one woman the whole time I was there. When I came home, I met another woman, who became my wife. We agreed that if there ever was a child born out of that relationship in Asia, we would adopt the baby."

He took a few gulps of air. "I want my son."

"Sir, you should do a blood test first."

"There's no reason. My girlfriend was faithful."

THE GIRL ON THE BANK

"Sir, I'd still advise that you take a blood test."

He finally agreed, and we arranged for him to be tested. I called him with the results. "Hans isn't your son."

"I don't care. I'll adopt him."

I knew that the man, as well intentioned as he was, was speaking out of emotion, not reason.

"Sir, take my phone number, and think about this. Call me back in three months if you still want to adopt him."

I never heard from the man again, but kudos to one of the few who wanted his child.

ॐॐॐ

A door opened, and I went through it ... on the other side were little lives that looked up with big smiles of thanks.

ॐॐॐ

Every time Greg and I visited the safe house, we would bring the children clothes, shoes and toiletries. We'd trace their feet on pieces of paper and use the markings to buy the right sizes.

One day, I asked a group of kids at the safe house to write down two or three things they would like to have. It was probably one of the hardest questions they'd ever been asked.

I handed out paper and pencils and told them not to talk until everyone had finished writing. I collected their answers and started reading.

CALLED TO RESCUE

"What do they say?" Greg asked.

"It's funny. There's one item that's the same on every paper. A towel."

A towel?

The next time we visited, we brought a rainbow assortment of towels. Each child chose his or her own color. We still could not comprehend how important they were to these children.

When we could secure U.S. passports for children, we would sometimes raise money for airline tickets and take them to the United States, where there would be more opportunity for education. Greg was in charge of ferrying three children to the airport in the Philippines late one night, and we asked the kids to pack the things they couldn't live without into 12- by 4-inch toy suitcases. They had to leave all of their extra clothes for the other kids.

The children dozed off in the van, and out of curiosity, Greg opened the three suitcases to see what they had packed. Each bag held one item.

A towel.

These kids had so little. They couldn't imagine anyone having the means to provide another new towel.

☙☙☙

People ask me, "Why do you feed street children? They are hungry again the next day." Yes, but they are not hungry that night. They are not hungry on my watch.

THE GIRL ON THE BANK

☙☙☙

While Greg and I visited Olongapo City when we could, I also turned my attention to Manila. I have a lot of energy and like to get things done. In Manila, I also needed to help children.

We lived within walking distance of one of Manila's grand cemeteries. The graves were above ground, and rows of tightly packed marble caskets were jammed close together on the property. Mausoleums and tropical trees were tightly mingled; at a distance the cemetery might look like a model of a city. I had often spotted kids running in and out of the cemetery's imposing 10-foot-high wooden gates.

Did they live there?

One day, I followed the children through the gate. As I stepped into the eerie world inside, the air was still and silent. *Where did they go?*

The cemetery had a million hiding places. Spaces between graves. Inside mausoleums. Behind trees.

All it took was a little time. I walked quietly through the graveyard, waiting them out. Out of the corner of my eye, I caught a movement behind a casket, then another. Curious children couldn't stay still, and soon we were engaged in a giant game of peek-a-boo as more and more curious faces popped up from hiding spots. I'm sure they wondered why a white woman was strolling by.

I stopped and smiled, hoping my expression would disarm any fear. The cemetery's residents — more than

200 adults and children — slowly emerged. They became my project.

My nearby neighborhood was filled with well-to-do families, and the wives of businessmen and employees of the embassy were happy to join me in my cause. We began to meet every week to assess the needs of the cemetery city and how we could help. We started with the children, cleaning them up and buying them books and uniforms for school. We enrolled them in the public school and paid their tuition.

I found a man who was paralyzed lying on a makeshift bed on the cold cemetery ground. He had a wife and five children. We took them on next. We bought stalks of bananas and taught them how to sell them on the street, creating a business and an income. We invested in bicycles with sidecars and helped the cemetery residents start a business taking fares and making money ferrying people around Manila. At Christmas, we took them presents. On occasion, the children from my subdivision would generously give up some of their gifts for their cemetery neighbors.

I learned that whatever you do to help others, you do it one person at a time. One kid to the safe house at a time. One kid from the cemetery into school at a time. One sick man to the hospital at a time. Taking on the world can be overwhelming. But caring for one person at a time can reap amazing change.

THE GIRL ON THE BANK

Three handsome, beautiful boys born to drug addicts and alcoholics. Did they ever stand a chance?

These three beautiful boys were sold for sex, sold for labor, sold and sold to provide alcohol and drugs for their parents. They were special, a sought-after commodity, because they looked alike, and there were three of them.

One evening, both parents were loaded, and they decided they didn't want the boys any longer. They decided to set them on fire. So they did. As the boys tried to put the fire out and free their bodies from the flames, they badly burned their hands and heads, leaving them scarred for life.

Called to Rescue jumped into action, saving them from further trauma. They now live in one of our safe houses and are slowly healing their internal scars, as well.

☙☙☙

As the years went by and I met more street children, the unfathomable truth became undeniably clear. Children were being bought and sold in staggering numbers, often by foreign men, for sex. They were being kidnapped and brutalized. Some were incomprehensibly young, forced to take part in the vile trade of child prostitution.

The stories I heard from children over the years composed a giant volume of evil in my mind. My anger grew at the "johns" who perpetuated the child sex trade. If there were no demand, there would be no business.

CALLED TO RESCUE

The statistics are hard to comprehend. More than $32 billion is made annually in the global trafficking of human beings. According to U.S. Department of Justice statistics from 2003, 1.2 million children are bought, sold or forced across the world's borders each year. Among them are hundreds of thousands of teenage girls and children as young as 5 years old.

My life's focus turned to rescuing and healing children. In 1992, I organized my work into *Called to Rescue*, a not-for-profit organization that saves children and teenagers from the sex trade, and five years ago, I returned to the United States to expand our efforts to address the problem of sex trafficking here, too.

☙☙☙

I still participate in our work in the Philippines, where my Filipino daughter-in-law handles many of our operations. At night, when I'm there, we often walk the red light districts, mixing into the sea of people flowing along the streets. People spill out of the bars and nightclubs, and men wave fliers advertising women who would like to provide "companionship."

The bars have names like "The Pussy Cat Club," and inside, men can have their choice of women, many who look suspiciously underage. The girls parade around in tight dresses or skimpy schoolgirl outfits; others wear nothing but a painted-on bikini. Girls as young as 8 or 9 years old are heavily made up to look older.

THE GIRL ON THE BANK

In one Filipino city, five blocks are cordoned off from traffic, and within those boundaries prostitution is legal. I've seen as many as 500 foreigners and 1,200 women and girls ambling down that street at any given time of the day.

I always carry business cards that read "Text Grammy." The safety and warmth of my own Grammy are some of my best memories, and I hope that the women and children who receive my cards perceive "Grammy" as a safe person they can call or text.

The cards are an easy way to slip contact information to people who want out of the sex trade without putting them in further danger. I often talk with girls and women I meet on the street, asking them if they are safe and if they want out. I offer to help. I offer them a different future.

When they take me up on it, I set a meeting time and place for the next morning, which allows me to work with the local authorities overnight and arrange for transit and a place for them to stay. Unfortunately, most change their minds and don't show up for our rendezvous.

Leaving the sex trafficking business isn't as clear-cut as it seems. Some girls make good money or have been brainwashed into believing they can't get out. Others are afraid — with good reason — of what pimps will do to their families if they run away.

One night I saw my bodyguards talking to a beautiful young girl outside a club. She had beckoned them over for business. The men I work with never go inside the clubs. "You need to stay here and talk to Grammy," I heard one of them say to the girl.

CALLED TO RESCUE

I walked over and touched her arm. After years of rescuing children in the Philippines, I could sense immediately that this one struggled with more complex issues of sexuality.

"You can get out *tonight*," I told her, looking right into her eyes. "I am here, and you can have a complete life change."

"I can't ..." She gulped out words and sobs. "I am a boy-girl."

"I don't care," I replied. I am in the business of saving children, including the transvestites or transsexuals who are part of the Asian sex business. "I am here to rescue you. I will be here tomorrow night at 8:00, and I will get you out. Meet me here."

He looked down and choked back his weeping. He already had made his choice.

The boy did not show up for the rescue. His pain was great. His embarrassment was clear. The money won.

One of my personal rules is that I never cry in front of other people. This job requires a tough skin, and there's a time and a place for emotional responses to the horrors I see.

A recent rescue, however, nearly brought me to tears before I could get alone.

A Filipino couple had left their daughters, ages 8 and 12, with a relative every day while they worked. The relative trafficked the girls in the sex trade, and the girls said nothing until the older sister could no longer watch her younger sister be abused. The 12 year old blew the

THE GIRL ON THE BANK

whistle, and I took them and their clueless parents to the authorities.

We agreed to meet the police at a local restaurant to discuss the case.

"What would they like to eat?" I asked the mom, nodding toward the girls as we chose a table.

She didn't know.

"How about some ice cream?"

The girls' big smiles were an easy answer. Their brown eyes lit up with the thought of the cold treat.

"What kind would you like?"

We ordered big scoops for each of them, and I sat back and watched the girls dig into it.

These kids are made for eating ice cream. They are not made for being trafficked by a 60-year-old man who is part of their family. Children should enjoy their childhood. This evil man has stolen that from these two.

I was overcome with the poignancy of watching two girls who had survived hell on earth joyously eating chocolate ice cream. Childhood should be so simple.

The tears came as soon as my car door shut. I leaned my head on the steering wheel and wept at the injustice, the horror of what these innocents and so many like them endured.

The sisters now live in one of our safe houses. It's near the beach, and they can walk to the water. The remodeled building has new paint, new bathrooms and a new kitchen. They will grow up there with a loving family of brothers and sisters and caregivers, and they will go to school and hopefully one day get married and work. We hope the beauty of the setting and the love and care they receive there will heal their young souls.

☙☙☙

"Greg, I need to go out on the street. Right now."

A weight that felt like a boulder was suddenly hanging from my heart and making it hard to breathe. It was 6:30 p.m. in Tijuana, Mexico, and we weren't scheduled to leave the hotel until 8 p.m. — with a fleet of six bodyguards wearing Kevlar and carrying M16s.

When we travel, we look for trafficked children, sometimes by just wandering the streets of cities. Revolution Avenue in Tijuana, once a hub for tourist shopping, has grown so dangerous that the local cops don't even venture onto it alone. They travel in packs of five or six, often on motorcycles, up and down the street packed with restaurants, shops and nightclubs.

"I just want to walk the street," I told Greg. "That's all I want to do. Maybe I just need to see the culture."

He agreed, even though a walk in this section of Tijuana by ourselves was a reckless proposition. I couldn't give him a logical explanation for my request.

As soon as we stepped out the hotel door onto the sidewalk, a Hispanic man turned the corner. He was gripping the upper arm of a pretty blond teenager. She was wearing jeans and a blouse with a white sweater slung around her shoulders. Had she been across the border,

THE GIRL ON THE BANK

where she'd probably come from, she easily could have been dressed to go to the mall with her friends.

The teenager forced the man to stop in front of us. She locked eyes with me.

"He's taken my papers. I have no ID. I have no money. You have to help me."

The man tried to pull her away, but she stayed planted. I tried to give her a reassuring look and speak calmly.

"That's what I'm here for. I'm here to help you."

"I can't get out of the country." Her blue eyes were pleading, but I could see a struggle behind them.

"I can walk you across the border. You need to come with me."

"But what about him?" She glanced at the guy who probably had assured her that he loved her deeply and wanted to take care of her forever.

Are you kidding? He's probably a pimp. Real boyfriends don't take your money and your identification!

I didn't have an answer for that, so I made one up. "You cannot get him into the United States if you are here, but if you are in the United States, you can bring him over." I had no idea if that was true, but she needed to get away from him.

The man pulled harder at the teenager's arm, trying to force her across the street.

"I'm going to call a cab," I told her. We needed a rescue vehicle. The man pulled harder. "Get your arm away from him! I am not going to take him on, but I will help you if you get away!"

CALLED TO RESCUE

She stared back and said nothing. Her arm hung limply at her side. I could see her slipping away.

"What's your name?" I begged for any scrap of information. "Where are you from? What state? Your parents want to know you're alive!"

As the man tugged on her harder, she and I cried. We both knew she should stay with me. Why wouldn't she pull away from this guy? *Answer my questions! I can help you!*

I shoved my "Text Grammy" card at her. She wasn't going to leave him.

"Memorize this number right now. Memorize it!"

She glanced down at the card as she let the man yank her into a hotel lobby across the street. I hung my head as she disappeared, probably forever, through the door.

I had vowed to Greg that I would never endanger my life in a rescue, so I didn't follow her.

The girl never said her name. I'm sure the man was a sex trafficker who sold her a story of love and commitment. He likely had no long-term intentions of loving her. It's a common line pimps use on unsuspecting young girls.

I reported the incident to the local police.

"We saw this girl," an officer told me the next day. "We see these girls all of the time."

⁂

THE GIRL ON THE BANK

More than 450,000 children run away in the United States each year, and at least 150,000 are trafficked, according to the U.S. State Department data from 2007. From my own experience, I believe that many of them are kept in the country. Most Americans don't realize how quickly they can lose a child to this depraved industry.

It can happen to any young person, regardless of his or her background, home life or socioeconomic status, and it can happen quickly. Places that seem safe, such as the mall or a fast-food restaurant, can be deceivingly dangerous.

Two 16-year-old girls recently decided to skip school one day. They headed to the nearest big city for a few hours of fun. Six hours after they pulled into the city, they were in a car with two 30-year-old men who had told them they loved them. Within 24 hours, the pimps had both teenagers working on the streets in another state.

Called to Rescue responds immediately to children's disappearances. It is vital that families be proactive, work with authorities and get on the street and look for their children. A pimp can change a child's appearance in minutes, making her unrecognizable to a rescue team with a picture. Family members can recognize a child by his or her walk.

We found these two teenagers by working with a phone company. I had one girl's mother call the company and insist that an employee call her when her daughter's cell phone came on and pinged. In the meantime, I organized a family search party on the streets of the city where the girls spent the day.

CALLED TO RESCUE

Five hours later, the phone company called back. The phone had pinged in a city 10 hours and two states away. We guessed they still were traveling in the same direction, and we were right. The police who found the girls on the street saved them from disappearing into the sex trafficking industry.

For children who are rescued from prostitution, it is vital to keep them away from their pimps. This can even mean moving or changing their names.

Our hotline number rang one day, and it was a girl who said one of her good friends had just returned home. The friend had been trafficked and wanted out, but a barcode had been tattooed on her neck — her pimp's version of branding his girls.

"How are we going to get that off her?" the caller asked.

The answer was complicated.

I asked where the girl lived. We chose a tattoo removal parlor in another city. We drove two cars. The people in the lead car checked out the place first, made sure it was safe and then parked and watched with cell phone ready to call the authorities if the pimp showed up. The second car carried the rescued girl, who went in for her appointment. As she left, the first car made sure she wasn't followed.

Those kinds of calls are normal for me.

Another family called with a daughter who had been pimped out to a man who had committed murder. The girl had somehow escaped back to her mom, and the mom felt like their house was being watched.

THE GIRL ON THE BANK

My advice?

"Put her in the floorboard of the backseat of your car. Take her far, far away. You'll need to keep her in school, but enroll her somewhere else and only use her middle name. Never use her first name again."

Because the pimp had killed someone before, the girl's entire family had to relocate. Staying where they were was too dangerous.

Pimps can employ all types of people and tricks to get girls. One woman, in her early 20s, had a good job and her own apartment. She walked her dog every morning at the same time, on the same route. Soon, another lady about her age began walking her dog. They talked almost every day as they walked, and they soon became good friends.

One day, the new friend mentioned that her lease was up on her apartment.

"I have a room in my apartment," the young woman offered. "You could move in with me."

"That would work out great!" the friend replied. "We can share the rent, and we'll both be in better shape."

The woman moved in, and within a few hours, an entire gang of people followed. They drugged the young woman and filmed her, and now the footage is on the Internet. When the girl disappeared, her family contacted *Called to Rescue* for help.

My police contacts followed every lead. We mobilized family and friends to search for her, but everything we tried came up empty. The only link we had remaining to the girl was her apartment, now occupied by a gang.

CALLED TO RESCUE

I suggested the family arrange stakeouts around the building, even though my gut told me the traffickers probably wouldn't bring the girl back there. But the parents wanted to do everything they could, so they set up outside their daughter's building. Within hours, they watched the traffickers bring their daughter back into her apartment.

What should I do now? The mom texted me.

Call the police, and tell them to come help you.

An officer in plainclothes knocked on the door, jammed his foot in when it opened and pulled the girl out by her arm. He threw her in the backseat of her dad's car.

"Buddy, drive," the officer ordered.

The dad started the car.

Where do we drive? The mom texted.

We have a safe house. Get on the highway, and don't stop until you get there.

I urge parents to watch over their children. Teach them how to defend themselves. Warn them about the tactics of evil people who can coerce them into the industry.

ॐॐॐ

At a recent *Called to Rescue* training session for volunteers, a woman asked me if I was trying to scare the group with stories of kidnapping, coercion and trafficking.

"Yes!" I replied.

I want people to understand that evil is a lot more evil

THE GIRL ON THE BANK

than they could possibly imagine. The depth of depravity in the world and the way that people with no conscience treat other human beings is difficult to comprehend. No one wants to think about something like human trafficking — until he or she is forced to.

We train volunteers to mobilize and search for victims and teach parents about the dangers that lurk everywhere. We want them to be aware of this wicked underworld so that they can protect their children.

Called to Rescue won't be satisfied with the rescue of hundreds or even thousands of children. We are taking on evil with everything we have and saving children, one at a time, from the horrors of sex trafficking.

CONCLUSION

I did not wake up one morning and say, "This is what I am going to do for the rest of my life; this is the cause I am going to fight." I just saw the need and did something about it.

The question I am asked the most is, "What can I, the normal everyday person, do?" Here is what I believe we can *all* do:

1. "Friend" *Called to Rescue* on your Facebook page (https://www.facebook.com/calledtorescue) and on Twitter (@calledtorescue) and "share" all missing children's information that comes to you.
2. Educate yourself and start telling everyone you know: a) Don't let your children go to malls alone (two children does not count as a group); and b) Get a team and do a "safety watch" at all the schools in your city.
3. Write letters to all legislators and get to know what is going on in your state, what the laws are and how they need to be changed. You have a voice and a vote. Use it! And then inform others so they know what the laws are.
4. Take and/or teach self-defense. Make sure your family members can defend themselves.

5. Google "missing children" in your area, and be on the alert.
6. Go online at www.calledtorescue.org and take our two Awareness Trainings.
7. If you would like to be a part of our *Civilian Task Force*, or get more information about it, go online and take the *Civilian Task Force* training and find out if this is something you would like to do. (You will need to eventually get your FBI background check to become an official member of a *Civilian Task Force*.)
8. Become an expert on human trafficking, and begin speaking out, to anyone and everyone who will listen. Go on radio and TV!
9. Plan a fundraiser so we can expand our dream of every child being free.
10. Share this book! Purchase it for friends and family. Pass it on.

IF YOU SEE SOMETHING YOU THINK IS SUSPICIOUS, DIAL 911 IMMEDIATELY.

After you have filed your police report, please use our hotline and call *Called to Rescue* so we can help you find your child.

***CALLED TO RESCUE* HOTLINE NUMBER: 1.855.646.5484**

Save this number in your cell phone right now. You never know when you may need it, when you will have the ability to save a life.

CONCLUSION

Please know that you can make a difference.
Thank you for helping to Defend the Defenseless.

Dr. Cyndi Romine
1.360.356.3761
www.calledtorescue.org
Info.calledtorescue@gmail.com

For more information on reaching your city with stories from your church, go to www.testimonybooks.com.

Good Catch Publishing

Did one of these stories touch you?
Did one of these real people move you to tears?
Tell us (and them) about it on our Facebook page!